Raising a Gifted Child

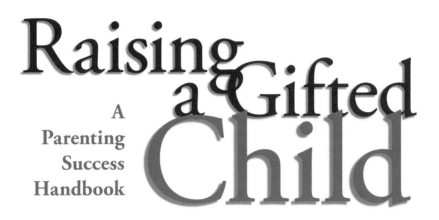

Raising a Gifted Child

A Parenting Success Handbook

CAROL FERTIG

PRUFROCK PRESS INC.
WACO, TEXAS

Library of Congress Cataloging-in-Publication Data

Fertig, Carol, 1945–
  Raising a gifted child : a parenting success handbook / Carol Fertig.
    p. cm.
  Includes bibliographical references.
  ISBN-13: 978-1-59363-344-8 (pbk.)
  ISBN-10: 1-59363-344-0 (pbk.)
  1. Gifted children. 2. Child rearing. 3. Parenting. 4. Gifted children—Psychology. 5. Gifted children—Education. I. Title.
  HQ773.5.F47 2009
  649'.155—dc22

                              2008034173

At the time of this book's publication, all facts and figures cited are the most current available. All telephone numbers, addresses, and Web site URLs are accurate and active. All publications, organizations, Web sites, and other resources exist as described in the book, and all have been verified. The author and Prufrock Press Inc. make no warranty or guarantee concerning the information and materials given out by organizations or content found at Web sites, and we are not responsible for any changes that occur after this book's publication. If you find an error, please contact Prufrock Press Inc.

Prufrock Press Inc.
P.O. Box 8813
Waco, TX 76714-8813
Phone: (800) 998-2208
Fax: (800) 240-0333
http://www.prufrock.com

To my parents, who always supported my interests,
and
To my two grown sons, whose creativity, resilience,
and passion for life are my inspiration.

CONTENTS

INTRODUCTION

RECENTLY, I was standing in line at the airport when a woman saw my carry-on bag with the words *Gifted Education* written across the side.

"Do you work with gifted children?" she asked. "I have a daughter who is in fifth grade but reads at a college level. Even though she is an outstanding reader, she doesn't meet the criteria for her school's gifted program. We don't know what to do with her."

I told her about the weekly blog I write at http://www.prufrock.com and suggested she could find lots of ideas there that might help her daughter both in and out of school.

"You mean my daughter doesn't need to be in a gifted program for us to get help?" she asked.

In the best of worlds, schools would attend to the needs of every child, no matter his or her ability. However, lack of funds, philosophical differences, insufficient teacher training, large class sizes, a wide variety of abilities within the classroom, and a host of other reasons often prevent this from being a reality. But this does not mean that parents should despair.

Families have power. Armed with appropriate knowledge and resources, parents and guardians can better navigate the maze of raising bright kids. Parents don't need to wait for others to make all of the decisions and then be frustrated if things don't work out.

You may advocate for change, but results often can take years. Highly able students need advanced learning and enrichment opportunities now!

The possibilities of providing for gifted kids are not limited to the schools—these possibilities extend as far as one's imagination is willing to travel. In addition, no matter how bad or good the opportunities at your child's school, there are many experiences that should still be provided at home.

Parents have the power to educate themselves about gifted issues, learn how to work positively with school systems, and ultimately take responsibility for the education of their sons and daughters. What often is missing is an understanding of how to find and tap into available resources.

There is no one way to define giftedness and no "correct" prescription for working with highly able individuals. Instead of giving you "magic" solutions in this book, I have provided a large menu of strategies, organizations, and Web sites to help you help your child learn and develop. You should pick and choose what works best for you and your family in the community in which you reside.

I encourage you to question and discuss philosophies of parenting and educating youngsters. I often pose questions, but do not necessarily provide answers. In the end, you and your family need to decide the answers and solutions that work best in your situation.

I hope you will find this book to be a valuable resource to which you will turn often. I also hope it will provide a basis for discussion in parent networking groups and with educators in the gifted community.

Although parenting is an enormous responsibility, it also is an experience to be cherished. You most certainly will be humbled as you make this journey. You want to help your children learn as they grow, but you also will find that you will grow as you learn from them.

1

WHO IS THIS KID ANYWAY?

WHAT DOES IT MEAN TO BE GIFTED?

THERE is no universal definition of the term *gifted*; instead, there are many different opinions. The last Friday of each month the gifted specialists in the school district where I worked met to talk about common issues. On one particular day, our discussion revolved around the meaning of the label *gifted*. Marsha commented that we (being specialists) all knew what the term meant. Someone in the group questioned that. So, we went around the table and stated just what gifted meant to each of us. Very quickly it became clear that we all had vastly different views.

Some perceived the term to mean high test scores, and some saw it as an unusual way of thinking. Some felt students needed to be considered advanced by several grade levels in all areas, while others considered it important to be advanced in only one subject. Some valued academics, and others valued visual-spatial strength or the arts. Some felt giftedness was determined by a given set of personality or emotional characteristics, while others thought it was exhibited when high grades and compliance came together to make the "perfect student." Some felt that one might be gifted for only a short time, while others felt it should last a lifetime. All of the specialists in this group had training in gifted education. Many had at least a master's degree in the field, yet we found that we did not have a common understanding of giftedness. Think of how confusing it must be to those who do not have any background in the field.

After working with classroom teachers and gifted education specialists across the country, I also can tell you that the term *gifted* often takes on different meanings in different environments. In some very high-level schools where most students work well above the norm for their age, the term gifted may take on a very different connotation than in a school where most students work well below the norm.

Looking beyond school, we see that strengths are valued differently in different societies. For example, in a society where people live off the land, being an excellent hunter or farmer will be valued far more than being able to read.

Even within our own cultural subsets some attributes are valued over others. What about sports or music or art or dance? What about leadership or mediation or oratorical skills? When looking at giftedness in a broad sense, it is not all about academics.

The problem is that the term gifted does not have a precise definition. If you talk to noted experts in the field, you will find many different nuances.

In addition, some people believe a youngster who is gifted will have the curiosity and tenacity to find his own way. Others feel that talent is lost if not appropriately nurtured—especially by the school system.

So, the experts debate questions like these:

- Is a person born gifted or can giftedness be developed at various points during one's life?
- Can we identify a person as gifted when he or she is young and expect that person to always behave in a gifted manner?
- Is one area of giftedness more important than another area?
- Should we expect schools to address all types of giftedness?

Given the philosophical differences that exist, it may be more productive to use specific descriptors rather than to say your child is gifted. It often is more helpful to know that the student has great insight into reading or has the ability to solve complex math problems in creative ways or is a great public speaker. It also is more meaningful to know a youngster is highly organized and goal oriented or is very sensitive to the feelings of others or is a wizard at science. By using specific descriptors, it may be easier for others to understand your child's needs and to give appropriate support.

Young people also may have personality traits that can cause them to look gifted or not gifted. For instance, some kids are very good students, because they learn how to play the parent or school game of pleasing others or following the rules. I can think of many kids who were shining stars all the way through high school. Often, their parents were vigilant, watching to make certain all homework assignments were completed on time and met high standards. Everyone seemed shocked when these same young people went away to college and, with no one to keep them on track, floundered.

Some students feel irritated with the ways in which they are asked to learn, rebelling against the system because they don't like authority or because their learning environment lacks challenge. Others have minds that truly work in different ways. They think "outside the box," question their environment, and make connections that others cannot.

The comparison list found in Table 1, first attributed to Janice Szabos (1989) in *Challenge Magazine* many years ago, has been adopted by many districts and individuals to explain the difference between a bright child and what some view as a gifted learner. It helps teachers and parents distinguish between strong, smart students and those who are truly unique. But, keep in mind that it is only one way to look at the term gifted.

TO TEST OR NOT TO TEST?

As parents (and teachers), we want to understand as much as possible about the individual children we work with so we can provide the best possible environment, enabling them to thrive both academically and emotionally. This is not always an

TABLE 1
A Bright Child vs. A Gifted Learner

A Bright Child:	A Gifted Learner:
Knows the answers	Asks the questions
Is interested	Is highly curious
Is attentive	Is mentally and physically involved
Has good ideas	Has wild, silly ideas
Works hard	Plays around, yet tests well
Answers the questions	Discusses in detail, elaborates
Top group	Beyond the group
Listens with interest	Shows strong feeling and opinions
Learns with ease	Already knows
Needs 6–8 repetitions for mastery	Needs 1–2 repetitions for mastery
Understands ideas	Constructs abstractions
Enjoys peers	Prefers adults
Grasps the meaning	Draws inferences
Completes assignments	Initiates projects
Is receptive	Is intense
Copies accurately	Creates a new design
Enjoys school	Enjoys learning
Absorbs information	Manipulates information
Is a technician	Is an inventor
Is a good memorizer	Is a good guesser
Enjoys straightforward sequential presentation	Thrives on complexity
Is alert	Is keenly observant
Is pleased with own learning	Is highly self-critical

easy task, but there are tools that can be helpful. Testing is one of those tools.

Ingrid was a confused parent. She wrote,

> I have a preschooler who is extremely smart. Most people say he is too smart. He is having a lot of behavior problems. The director at his school thinks he is gifted. Many others have said he probably has ADHD, but I don't believe it. Can you please point me in some direction to have my son tested and also to find schools that specialize in gifted and talented? I am lost. I am a desperate mother with a beautiful and bright child who just needs some special attention.

This mother obviously loves her son very much and wants to find the best possible environment for him. She wants more information to determine if his capabilities are as high as she thinks and also if there is a misfit with his environment, causing his behavior problems. Testing is one tool that might be used, but we must remember that test scores only offer us one piece of the puzzle to understanding the makeup of each individual child.

There are many different types of assessments available, each with a specific purpose, including achievement tests, IQ tests, and emotional/behavioral assessments.

Schools generally have all children take one or more achievement tests to determine if the students understand the grade-level curriculum they have been taught. These tests are administered to the entire class and they measure what your child has already learned, not your young person's abilities. Even within the category of achievement tests, it can be confusing—especially when a child is given several different achievement tests and scores vary widely within a given subject area. Understanding exactly what each test measures and the types of questions on each instrument is important. For instance, in the area of math, one test may measure computation, another problem solving, and another visual-spatial ability. So, a child may score high on a subtest of computation, indicating that he knows his math facts, yet score low on the problem-solving subtest, indicating he has difficulty reasoning through real problems. For better understanding, ask the administrator of the assessments for an explanation of the school tests and how they will be used.

Intelligence (IQ) tests are designed to determine a child's ability or potential (i.e., assess innate ability rather than what he has already learned). These tests need to be administered individually, one on one. More often than not, parents who want their child to have an IQ test need to go outside of the system and pay to have the test administered. It usually is beyond a school's budget to give IQ tests whenever requested.

There also are behavioral assessments that can be given by psychologists to help determine if behavioral issues are due to biological problems, educational settings, lack of self-control, inappropriate discipline, and so forth.

Ingrid, the mother who was very confused about the behavior and abilities of her son, may find that both intellectual and behavioral evaluations administered by a professional would help her better understand her child's strengths and provide her with recommendations for the best educational environment.

Other parents may have different reasons to go through a testing process. Some need to supply a minimum aptitude score for their child to enter a gifted program at school. Still others see that their child is very bright but also has some significant learning problems. They want an evaluation with suggestions for helping the child work on both strengths and challenges. Finding a qualified person to provide an appropriate evaluation for any of these dilemmas may be a difficult hurdle.

Before having your child individually evaluated, ask yourself some questions. Will a certain score make different educational options available? Will it cause you to look at your child differently? Will your expectations for your child change? Would that change be beneficial or detrimental to the child? At best, test scores only should be used as one piece of a puzzle in assessing a child's ability. For example, adults may have difficulty understanding a child who has a high IQ but is not motivated to use that ability.

When privately assessing the abilities of highly able youngsters, it is best to find a psychologist who has worked with gifted children who are the same age as your child. The evaluator should be experienced in ascertaining various levels of high intelligence and the pros and cons of the spectrum of tests available. Find out what tests will be used and how the information will be presented to you. If your young person needs to provide a score on a specific test to be admitted to a gifted program, make certain the appropriate test will be administered. Also be sure that the psychologist will make educational recommendations to guide you. Different levels of intelligence require different approaches. A student who is deemed gifted may require one level of education while a prodigy requires something quite different. The psychologist should understand your purpose for testing.

To begin a search for psychologists in your geographic area, look at:

- National Association for Gifted Children (NAGC)—http://www.nagc.org (click on Gifted by State)

  Here you will find contact information for both your state gifted association and the gifted arm of your state department of education. Discussing your needs with people at either of these organizations may produce recommendations.

- Hoagie's Gifted Education Page: Psychologists Familiar With Testing the Gifted and Exceptionally Gifted—http://www.hoagiesgifted.org/psychologists.htm

  This Web site includes several articles explaining things to consider when choosing a psychologist to test children, ways to use test information, and names of specific psychologists who have experience working with gifted young people.

Understanding the purpose and scores of all tests administered to a child may be beneficial, but parents need to remember that they also need to look at their student's personality characteristics, learning styles, and general environments.

WHERE DID THIS CHILD COME FROM?

Often parents are surprised by their children.

"I think I must have picked up the wrong baby at the hospital," stated one mother, when talking about her elementary school whiz kid. She had no idea how her daughter knew the things she did or how she developed her interests. Kim seemed so much more alert than most babies from the very beginning, focusing her eyes on objects almost from the time she was born and not wanting to sleep as much as the baby books predicted. By the age of 2, she had taught herself to read simple books. By the time she entered kindergarten, Kim could read anything and was a walking encyclopedia of facts. She was especially fond of science and carried a magnifying glass in her pocket so she could look more carefully at bugs when she encountered them or look more intricately at the patterns in leaves and other things she found outdoors. Where did these abilities and interests originate?

Parents may be confused and bewildered by their kids, especially when their interests, abilities, and personality characteristics are very different from those of the rest of the family. For instance, the Prichard family in Colorado built their lives around outdoor activities, camping every weekend in the summer, and skiing or snowshoeing every weekend in the winter. The parents were intensely interested in understanding all aspects of nature: the flora, the fauna, and how to "rough it." It surprised them when neither of their children was interested in these things. Instead, one only wanted to play the clarinet and the other was interested in computer programming. Should the Prichards expect their children to follow the family tradition of outdoor living or support their kids' individual interests?

Some very bright youngsters may be well-rounded, academically strong, athletically adept, musically inclined, and able to get along well with others. Some children may not. Should parents and teachers push kids to broaden their interests or allow them to develop their own areas of expertise?

Parents may find that their kids jump from one area of interest to another, seemingly unable to stick with any one thing. Must we require them to stay with an activity once they begin it or should we assume this is just a time of experimentation? All of these questions must be pondered, but again, there are not necessarily correct answers.

WHAT IS THE "RIGHT" CHOICE?

Life is like a *Choose Your Own Adventure* story. This popular children's series from the 1980s is an analogy for the alternatives with which we are presented each day. All readers start at the beginning of a book, but after a few pages choices need to be made. Perhaps the story is about a child who decides to go to the circus. After a few pages, the youngster is given a choice. Does he want to go to the big top or to the sideshow? If you, as the reader, want him to go to the big top, you turn to page 14. If you want him to go to the sideshow, you turn to page 25. After reading a few more pages, you are given another option, and another, and another. The book can be read over and over again, each time with a different result. The endings are not necessarily bad; they just have different outcomes—or, in some cases, you may take several different paths and still come out with the same result.

I've often thought how much *Choose Your Own Adventure* stories are like life. We face choices all the time. Some are more serious than others, but with each choice, our life takes a slightly different turn. As parents, I think we often get caught in the trap of thinking there is only one correct way of "reading the book" of raising our kids. We are afraid that if we don't move into the right neighborhood or choose the right school or the right teacher for our kids the results will be devastating. To avoid this we often feel that we need to place a value judgment on each alternative—If my child doesn't take these classes, future doors of opportunity will be shut forever. If I can't convince my child's teacher to put my daughter in a different reading group, she will be destined to unhappiness. Although there's a slight chance this may be true, it is much more likely that each result will just be different—not necessarily better or worse. There may even be some positive consequences that surprise you.

Although we may want to have control over everything that happens, we usually do not. We do, however, have control over how we react to situations and the lessons to be learned as we parent our sons and daughters. So, as you read this book, try to see the many paths that may be taken and do not get hung up on thinking there is only one correct way. If Plan A doesn't work, try Plan B.

We get caught up in the perfectionism of parenting because we're afraid we might ruin the lives of our gifted kids. We also don't want to be considered failures as parents. Instead of becoming insistent that everything happen "just so," I recommend relaxing a bit and considering what good may come out of a situation that doesn't look favorable on the surface. For instance, if not placed in a perfect situation, will your child learn some coping skills? May he find a way to become more self-reliant? Will she be exposed to some ideas that could lead her down an exciting path that you would not have been able to provide? It's often one's attitude toward different choices that can be more important than the choice itself.

As kids get older and more independent, you may find that they make choices that are not OK with you. Sometimes, very bright students choose not to go on to college or they pass up a traditional job. The parents wring their hands and feel like failures. In many of these cases, these kids are just taking non-traditional paths. As one parent put it, "My son decided to retire at the age of 22." For years he wandered, seeming to do nothing with his life. Now, at 27, he's in a Ph.D. program.

Owen is a good example of this kind of thinking. After high school, Owen would get menial jobs and sleep on a friend's couch so he could save all of his money to travel. He traveled to the most exotic places, stayed with the native people under primitive conditions, and quickly learned the language of each place he visited. Somewhere along the line, he became interested in photography and then macro photography. He wound up going back to school and becoming an entomologist. Now he is working on a Ph.D., and although it has taken him until the age of 32 to get there, think of the life experiences he had that the rest of us missed.

So, don't lose faith if parenting your gifted student has its ups and downs and if you aren't always able to make things work for your child. Your family may be taking an unexpected path, but that doesn't mean it will have undesirable results in the end.

WHICH REAL WORLD?

When Josh and Brad were young, full of energy, and often expressing their creativity in nontraditional ways, teachers would say to their parents, "Your sons need to be more (fill in the blank: organized, settled down, compliant, and so forth) because when they get out into the real world . . ."

Josh and Brad's parents often asked themselves, "Which 'real world' is this person talking about?" Is it one in which a worker needs to adhere to a strict time schedule or a job where he might work out of his home, in his pajamas, at midnight? Is it one where specific paperwork needs to be turned in on a regular basis or one where more creative thought is valued? Is it one where technology is considered only a tool or one where technology is one's livelihood? Is it one where interpersonal skills are mandatory or one where self-discipline is needed for solitary work? There are so many real worlds out there. Schools traditionally address only a few of them.

School skills are very important, but there also are many valuable traits that are developed beyond the everyday curriculum. There are conventional paths that children may follow, but there also are many exciting nonconventional paths they may take. Each child is different, each family is different, and each environment is different. Just as the teachers sometimes questioned the skills Josh and Brad needed, many times their mom and dad questioned their own parenting skills. Just like you, they wanted their sons to be happy, thoughtful, resilient individuals who would become contributing citizens of the world. However, to the parents, the details of how their sons achieved this status in life were not as important as just getting there in the end. How can anyone believe that kids need to follow a specific path? How could anyone know if a specific direction would lead to one's ultimate goal?

Parenting is all about preparing children to become successful adults who can make decisions that are physically, intellectually, and emotionally healthy. This may not occur according the path that you have imagined.

In this book, I provide tools and resources to help you see the possibilities of the many paths that may be taken to provide for the education of your gifted child.

CONCLUSION

We often are most comfortable when we can fit our thoughts into neat little boxes, but as you can see, it is difficult to do that when discussing the term *gifted*. The word has too many meanings.

Parents often ask how their children can be identified for gifted programs at school. First of all, many schools do not have gifted programs or, if they do, the programs do not start until third or fourth grade. In addition, the identification process varies widely from state to state and often from school to school. Because of varying criteria, a student may be identified as gifted at one school but not another.

Instead of focusing on the label of "gifted" and insisting that their children be labeled as such, I highly recommend that parents focus on their kids' strengths and challenges. These strengths and challenges can be met by choices that you make at home, ways in which you work with the schools, and lifestyle decisions. There are many ways to meet the educational and emotional needs of your children. My goal is to provide you with an array of ways to look at and try to understand your children, as well as a menu of resources with which to work.

2

UNDERSTANDING GIFTED KIDS

ALTHOUGH experts cannot agree on a precise definition of the word *gifted*, there are general traits we can talk about. How we view those traits as parents can make a big difference to kids.

GOING FORTH WITH A POSITIVE ATTITUDE

So many general advertisements seen in the media are designed to instill fear. I get a regular ad from my energy company telling me about the number of appliances that break down each year. They urge me to buy their insurance plan so I can put my mind at rest. I get ads telling me that my car is no longer under warranty. If I would only purchase a specific plan, I could avoid big expenses should anything major go wrong. Everywhere I turn, I am told if I don't do XYZ then something terrible will happen.

This negative viewpoint also is used with gifted kids. For example, Rosita's mom made an appointment to see the gifted and talented teacher at her child's school. The fourth grader was a delightful young lady who was an excellent student and well-liked by her peers. Rosita's mom, however, was very concerned because she had read articles stating that both gifted girls and gifted minority students are "at risk." She wasn't even sure what at risk meant, but she was convinced that because her daughter was a girl and also an ethnic minority that terrible things would happen and she wanted the teacher to do something about it.

Henry loved to participate in intellectual discussions, especially about science. He also had a wonderful singing voice and was active in the Children's Chorale, which performed with the symphony orchestra several times a year. His parents had read that many gifted kids have social problems. They were concerned because Henry's interests were different from most of his classmates. His parents were concerned that he would be looked upon as an oddity.

Whether it is meant to or not, at least some research on gifted education has the potential to instill fear in parents. We read that gifted children may have certain personality characteristics that can cause serious problems, such as feeling different from peers, lacking tolerance of others, and experiencing intensities that cause higher rates of depression and put them at greater risk of suicide. Parents are led to imagine scenarios about gifted personality characteristics, which sometimes become self-fulfilling prophecies because of the subtle messages they wind up giving their kids.

The truth is that gifted kids, like any other segment of the population, may or may not have characteristics that cause distress. Although it is important for parents to be aware of red flags, bad things should not be expected. The term *at risk* often is used in education today, but we have to be careful with its application.

Yes, I am at risk that one of my major appliances may break down. Yes, I am at risk of having something go wrong with my car. But that doesn't mean I should I walk around every day expecting something to go wrong. I choose whether or not to live in fear and how much energy I want to spend worrying about these things that may never happen. Isn't it a better use of my time to create a beautiful yard by planting flowers or a calming home by decorating a room than to fear what might go wrong?

All kids are at risk of something going wrong and all need support. So, if a personality characteristic or other social-emotional influence affects your child—gifted or not—yes, you should be there to help him out. But also be careful not to expect bad things to happen.

For families of gifted children, knowledge is power. The following sections describe some of the characteristics of gifted children and how we might view them in positive ways.

WHEN GOOD IS BAD AND BAD IS GOOD

Every personal characteristic has its good points and its bad points. Sometimes the same traits that are valued in one situation are considered negative in another situation. This is certainly true with gifted individuals. We call these good/bad traits *concomitant characteristics.* Table 2 shows some of these characteristics.

People often have strengths that work very well for them in certain settings, but work against them in other settings. For example, Frank, a surgeon, had been having some problems with his family.

"They get upset with me," he said, "not only because I want things done a certain way, but when I ask that something be done, I expect it to be done immediately."

When Frank makes decisions, he sees no reason why everyone shouldn't agree that his decisions are correct. When things don't go as he expects, he lets his wife and kids know about it: "I realize that I may do and say things that irritate other people," he continued, "but when I'm in surgery, I *have* to make snap decisions and I *need* for things to be done well and done quickly. Those characteristics are essential for me there."

Frank was right. The ability to make decisions, to give commands, and have everyone jump to his beckoning is vital in the operating room. It does not, however, work so well in the home environment.

Maria, a fifth grader, was a voracious reader. Given a choice, she would read from the time she woke up in the morning until she went to bed at night. Although pleased that she was able to read many grade levels above her peers, her parents were concerned because she seemed to have no other interests. She did not interact much with friends or family. She was not interested in sports or musical instruments or hobbies or even

TABLE 2
Concomitant Characteristics of Gifted Kids

Characteristic	Positive Aspect	Negative Aspect
Verbal proficiency	Articulates well	Dominates the conversation
Accelerated pace of learning	Moves through material quickly	Gets frustrated with the pace of learning
Ability to concentrate and persist	Focuses on a task and learns in depth	Resists interruption
Seeks order	Plans ahead and keeps everything neat	Has difficulty with spontaneity
Sense of humor	Is entertaining and resilient	Uses humor in inappropriate ways that distract or offend
Heightened self-awareness; feels different	Realizes the potential of being unique	Feels isolated and self-consciousness
High expectations	Sets high standards	Criticizes self and/or others when high expectations are not met
Self-confident, leader	Influences others	Perceived as bossy
Huge store of facts and long memory	Learns quickly	Becomes bored and impatient with others
Creative	Thinks innovatively	Disrupts with his innovation
Many interests	Has many possibilities in life	Has difficulty choosing between interests
Goal oriented	Gets tasks done	Viewed as stubborn and inflexible
Deep thinker	Conceptualizes on a greater level	Hates deadlines because they infringe on her process of analyzation
Perfectionist	Does everything well	Avoids tasks for fear of not doing them perfectly

TV. Sometimes, it was difficult to get her to stop reading and join the family at the dinner table.

Dakota, an eighth grader, was very creative. He constantly found new uses for ordinary objects and had a vivid imagination. Those are great qualities, but they often caused him problems in school. When he got bored in class, he drew cartoons. Those cartoons were often very irreverent portrayals of his teachers. When his math teacher discovered his drawings, Dakota was immediately sent to the dean's office for discipline.

Leticia was academically strong in all areas and was very active in extracurricular activities, both at school and in the community. She constantly struggled with time. Her interests were very broad and she wanted to "do it all," but there were only so many hours in the day. What suffered was her sleep. Leticia also experienced a lot of stress in choosing a college major. She could have been very successful in a number of different fields but struggled to make a choice. How could she possibly reach a decision?

Think about people you know—both adults and children. What traits do they have that work both to their advantage *and* to their disadvantage? Think about yourself. Is this true for you as well?

What about the person who talks your ear off? Perhaps that person would be a good public speaker. Think of the student who is the class clown. Could that person grow up to become the next great stand-up comedian? What about the child who always asks questions and never seems to be satisfied with the answers? Will she take her questioning into the world of science and discover great things? If you look at people with this understanding, will you see that there are two sides to every coin? Will it help you to steer your child in directions where that potentially negative characteristic might be used in a more positive environment?

We should never make excuses for a youngster's poor behavior, but we can try to help the child by understanding some of the stresses that he may experience with concomitant characteristics and help steer him in directions where these attributes can work to his advantage.

If we can help young people better understand themselves, we also can help them figure out where they might best use the positive aspects of those characteristics in future occupations. At the same time, through self-awareness, we can work to temper those characteristics in situations where they may be offensive.

THE PERILS OF PERFECTIONISM

There is one concomitant characteristic to which parents need to pay special attention—perfectionism. There is a fine line between striving for excellence and pushing oneself into an unhealthy state of high expectation.

As a passenger on an airplane, I want to have a pilot who knows exactly what to do in any situation. If I hire a lawyer, I want him to attend to every element of my situation. We look for people at our workplace to not only be bright, but also dedicated, with attention to detail. We applaud the student who studies hard, does excellent work, and is never a behavior problem.

One would think, then, that trying to be perfect is a highly desirable trait. Unfortunately, perfectionism also can have its downsides—especially for gifted students.

When Bjorn was only 3 years old, he wanted to learn how to make his bed. His mother taught him and he did a good job; however, if he couldn't make it without a wrinkle, he would be very upset with himself. He had a habit of taking his open hand and slowly moving it down his face, over and over again. He thought that if he kept making that movement, he would keep the tears from welling up in his eyes.

When Bjorn was 6, he wanted to learn to play the piano. When he played his simple pieces, it was important to him to play them perfectly. If he made a mistake, his hand again would slowly start moving down his face. It was very upsetting to his parents to see him so stressed out.

Finally, when he was about 8, this need for perfectionism started to turn. Suddenly (for no obvious reason), he didn't keep everything in his room tidy. Although many mothers might have called the child to the room and asked him to straighten it up, Bjorn's mother was secretly doing a little dance in her head.

When Bjorn, who had continued to work hard at the piano, chose a college, he rejected the possibility of a 4-year, fully paid music scholarship at one school so that he could attend a more difficult school. A couple of months into his freshman year his parents asked him how it was going. He replied, "I'm the worst pianist here." Their hearts sank and his dad said, "That must feel terrible." Bjorn's voice took on an enthusiastic tone as he boasted, "No. Not at all. It gives me something to work toward."

Over the years, Bjorn had learned to change from striving for perfectionism (something unattainable and frustrating) to a person who strove for excellence (attainable, gratifying, and healthy). In other words, he set high goals and worked toward them, but didn't get upset if he didn't do as well as he hoped. He became realistic in his objectives.

Many young people who are perfectionists are consumed by fears, especially fears of social, academic, or parental rejection. These children perceive themselves as failures, feeling they have not met either their own expectations or the expectations of others. They may feel that respect and love from others is conditional upon their performance. Every situation is all or nothing, black or white. They feel that they must be their best at all times and perform at the highest levels.

Surprisingly, effects of perfectionism also may be exhibited by either starting a task and not finishing it or not even attempting a task, such as in these examples:

- Samantha's seventh-grade locker was filled with homework assignments that she had never handed in to her teachers.
- Even though he was very capable, Zach never signed up for advanced classes.
- Penelope knew she had a looming school project on the horizon, but kept postponing its start.

Perfectionists many not begin or complete their work when they feel they won't be the best. They reason that by not trying to finish or start a task, they have no risk of failing at the completed task—in other words, they can make the excuse for failure that they *chose* not to or didn't want to participate.

When external pressures (either real or perceived) are exerted upon some children, results can be even more acute. These external pressures may include due dates, reward systems, and expectations for certain grades. Although these pressures work to the advantage of many students, they may cause problems for students who are extremely sensitive. We need to help students with their perceptions.

Here are some strategies for dealing with perfectionism in kids:

- Discuss perfectionism with your young person—its symptoms, causes, and misconceptions.
- Share stories that show that mistakes can be used as learning tools. Look at any book about inventors or athletes and you will find stories of people who failed many times for every success they experienced.
- Help kids determine the areas of their lives that they can control and those that they cannot.
- Help students to self-evaluate, drawing attention to their strengths and accomplishments, and to reinforce progress they make toward goals.
- Make certain children know that you love them unconditionally, not just for what they accomplish.
- Be a good role model: Demonstrate that learning is a process of trial and error. Stay with problems for a reasonable amount of time, even if the problems are difficult. Admit your own mistakes. Model your own

imperfect behavior, self-evaluation process, goal setting, reasonable risk-taking, and self-acceptance of your own imperfections and "off" days.

- Encourage and expect children to try new things.
- Help your young person look for realistic standards.
- If a child perceives that she has failed at something, wait until after the emotional tension is reduced before discussing the matter.
- Teach admiration as a strategy for handling jealousy by noticing, admiring, and communicating admiration to others. When playing games together, voice appreciation for the skill used in a particular move rather than being upset that the person is beating you.

Children may place unrealistic expectations on themselves. Parents and teachers often comment that they don't understand where these unrealistic expectations come from as the adults are not pushing the child in any way (or do not realize they are pushing the child). Sometimes we don't know the origins of these self-imposed demands, but for bright kids they do exist. Always having to be the best can have devastating effects on one's self-esteem. Unrealistic expectations may lead to negative perfectionistic tendencies rather than striving for excellence.

Kids need help understanding that there are different ways to approach life and different ways to look at experiences—that they do have choices and the ability to control many things in their lives and that there are tools and coping strategies that can be used to affect their lives in positive ways.

ACADEMICALLY ADVANCED BUT SOCIALLY IMMATURE

Some gifted students may be academically advanced, yet socially immature. When children are verbally precocious and have a broad base of knowledge, we often assume that they automatically will develop personal and social skills. If the skills do not come automatically, we excuse them, saying it is because they are so gifted and others don't understand them.

Javier was a very articulate second grader, and his reading level was several years ahead of his age peers. The boy was fluent in both English and Spanish and was learning Portuguese. He couldn't understand why his parents and brother were not able to learn the third language as quickly as he did. Actually, Javier was irritated with his parents because he didn't even feel they had a good command of the English language.

Even beyond languages, science was Javier's real love, so it was arranged for the gifted resource teacher at his school to pull him out of class a couple times a week to work on the subject. When pulled out, Javier never thought to say a proper hello or good-bye to the adult who was working with him. If he did not like a particular project they were going to work on, he would let it be known in no uncertain terms with words like "stupid" and the condescending expression, "Oh, please. This is just too much!" Although Javier was a very bright child, he lacked social graces and tolerance of other people. No adult had directly approached his social skills because they were all intimidated by Javier's general intelligence and ability to articulate.

By excusing social skills, we do kids a disservice. We send them off into the world ill-equipped. Social skills should be taught explicitly. No matter how bright the young person, we often must teach the simplest things, such as:

- introducing oneself,
- saying hello and good-bye courteously,
- when to listen and when to talk,
- telephone skills,
- table manners,
- appropriateness of language and topics of conversation with different groups,
- ways to include other people in a conversation or play activity,
- how to get along with many types of people,
- tolerance for different individuals and ideas, and
- acceptance of constructive criticism.

Even after these most basic skills have been taught, one shouldn't take for granted that they will be used automatically. Compliment your child when you see him use a skill effectively. When he doesn't do a good job, wait until you are in private and ask if there is another way the situation could have been handled. Practice these basic skills at home.

EXTROVERT VS. INTROVERT

In society today there is a great emphasis on being social and having lots of friends, but some people savor being alone

TABLE 3
Typical Characteristics
of Extroverts and Introverts

Extrovert	Introvert
Is sociable, outgoing	Desires private space and time
Enjoys interaction with others	Is happy to be alone—can become drained around large groups of people
Prefers to work in a group	Prefers to work alone
Is expressive	Is reserved, quiet, and deliberate
Likes being center of attention	Is content to be on the sidelines
Thinks out loud	Thinks carefully before speaking
Likes people a lot and wants to be liked in return	Forms a few deep attachments
Hates to do nothing	Needs time alone to recharge batteries

and are most productive in this state. Your child may be one of these people.

There are many ways to consider learning styles and personality types. One way is to classify a person as either an *extrovert* or an *introvert*. Table 3 provides some typical characteristics of introverts and extroverts. The extrovert's main interests are with the outer world of people and things, while the introvert is more involved with the inner world of concepts and ideas. Well-developed introverts can deal competently with the world around them when necessary, but they do their best work inside their heads, in reflection. Just like other traits, there are positive and negative aspects to being either an extrovert or introvert.

Many teachers (and parents) are extroverts, and it often is very difficult for an extrovert to understand an introvert. Therefore, an adult may see the introverted student as someone with a problem, not as simply someone with a different personality type. This misunderstanding may lead to attempts to get the young person to be "friendlier," to work in large groups, to talk more often and more spontaneously, and to be more outgoing and interactive.

There is nothing wrong with being an introvert. It does not need to be cured. Although adults need to be able to tell when the introversion (or extraversion) is dysfunctional, in most cases introverted students don't need to be changed to match other students. So, don't try to change kids who are introverts. Don't assume there is something wrong with them. There are many advantages to being introverted. Introverts (1) don't always need to have people around; (2) are quite happy to entertain themselves or to learn on their own; and (3) are potentially more productive, because they can get right to the task at hand rather than being distracted by others.

ASYNCHRONOUS DEVELOPMENT

Madison taught herself to read simple books when she was 3. She became interested in numbers when she was 4 and started doing simple addition and subtraction problems. By the time she entered kindergarten she was reading chapter books and doing two-digit addition and subtraction. Her parents felt she could handle at least first grade and possibly second grade. However, although they realized that she was advanced academically, they also realized she was well behind her age peers in other respects. She had difficulty putting on her own coat: Her fine motor skills seemed delayed, making it difficult for her to draw or write, and she cried much too easily. Madison experienced asynchronous development.

Asynchronous development is uneven development academically, physically, and/or emotionally. A student might be a whiz kid at science, but can't throw a ball; or she may read years ahead of her classmates, but perform at grade level in math.

We often expect children to meet certain developmental standards. We know they should begin to crawl by a certain age, then go on to walk and run. We expect them to communicate using sentences when the baby books say they should. We are given guidelines when young people should recognize colors and shapes, begin to read, learn to share toys, and so forth. Educators have both academic and social expectations at each grade level. But, children do not necessarily develop just as anticipated.

Few children meet benchmarks across all areas in each year of school; however, disparity in development can be exacerbated when a child has especially high abilities in one or more academic areas. A wide discrepancy of abilities is especially difficult for teachers in primary grades (K–3) because the same child who excels academically may not be mature enough for independent work. At the lower grades, students need constant supervision. It can be very hard for the teacher to modify curriculum to meet the needs of a child with high academic performance because it is likely that same child will still need an adult to supervise her outside of the main group.

Parents and teachers may need to get very creative when trying to meet the needs of young children with asynchronous development. A combination of techniques may be employed, including the use of volunteers in the classroom, moving students to a higher grade for part of the day, and small-group work with motor and social skills.

NOT ALL MADE FROM THE SAME MOLD

There is no cookie-cutter description for a gifted child; they come in many different shapes and sizes. Here are just a few examples divided into areas of strength, learning timelines, levels of energy, levels of sensitivity, and absorption of material.

Areas of Strength

- Ethan is gifted in many areas. Everything comes easily to him. He gobbles up knowledge in all areas, is self-motivated, is a good athlete, and gets along well with others.
- Alexis has excellent leadership skills and is great with both intrapersonal and interpersonal skills, but is pretty average academically.
- Andrew plays the violin beautifully and is strong in mathematics, but is a below-average reader.

Gifted kids may be good at everything, have strengths in just one or two areas, or excel in many areas with a couple of peaks or valleys.

Learning Timelines

- Benjamin questions everything and does not like to be told what to do. He does not fit well into the school system, yet as an adult goes on to be the CEO of a large corporation.
- Samantha starts out as an average student. In fourth grade everything suddenly begins to click. Samantha now suddenly loves learning, works hard, and becomes the top student in her class.
- Lauren graduates as valedictorian from her high school and then completes 4 years at a prestigious college. Once she graduates, she is satisfied with a job that requires none of her academic skills.

Gifted kids may be very good students but do little with their academic abilities later in life. They may perform poorly in school and then go on to achieve as adults. They may develop midway through their academic careers.

Levels of Energy

- Noah responds very well to rules and always is anxious to please those around him—especially adults. He is the model, hardworking student.

- Ella's teachers wish that she would just sit still and be quiet for 2 minutes. It feels like she "bounces off the walls." She obviously is smart, but unless she learns to harness her energy, she will never experience success.
- Logan often seems lethargic, yet when asked about topics in which he is interested, he provides thoughtful, in-depth comments.

Gifted kids may be energetic to the point of distraction, have very low energy, or be the model student. Sometimes this excessive energy is attributed to Attention Deficit/Hyperactivity Disorder by school staff. However, there can be other reasons for such variances in energy, including enthusiasm for the subject at hand, boredom, lack of level of challenge, or a learning disability that precludes the child from understanding and engaging in all of the information.

Levels of Sensitivity

- Sensitivity is Natalie's forte. She is acutely aware of the body language and voice modulation of others. She is a good listener and wonderful friend.
- Christian could care less what anyone else thinks or feels about anyone. He just wants to be left alone so he can work on his special interests.
- William is very intelligent, but because of his misplaced humor, his anger, and his asocial behavior, his teachers fear that he may eventually commit a criminal act.

Gifted kids may be very sensitive to others, insensitive, or downright asocial. Many experts note that gifted kids often are highly sensitive to global issues such as war or poverty, taking an absorbed interest in the plights of others and wanting to help.

Absorption of Material

- Nicholas hears or reads something once and it is embedded in his mind. He is a walking encyclopedia.
- Chloe takes a great deal of time to process new material, but once she thoroughly absorbs and analyzes it, she knows it well.
- Although Mia is able to thoroughly understand anything she reads, she learns little from listening to people convey knowledge.

Gifted kids may process material very quickly or process material slowly but thoroughly. They also may have very specific learning styles. Golon (2008) provides a nice resource on visual-spatial learners, one type of learning style of many gifted kids. Generally, these children learn well from doing, rather than hearing. They can look at a machine, such as a computer, and take it apart and put it back together. Other children learn best by hearing or reading information directly. Ask your child what helps her learn something new and try to develop strategies to help her use those strengths to her advantage.

CONCLUSION

Although many lists of gifted traits have been published, it's a rare child who is cut from the predetermined mold of a list. It's important to remember that your child may exhibit intelligence differently than the next child. Knowing the many possible characteristics of able individuals will help you to better understand your student, create realistic expectations, and help your young person develop the skills necessary for a fulfilling life.

3

EXPECTATIONS

SOPHIA, a single mother, needed to have the exterior of her house painted. A well-meaning gentleman down the road couldn't understand why she didn't save some money and have her teenage boys do the job. For some reason, her neighbor assumed that, because they were boys, they were born with the necessary skills to paint a house. No one had taught the kids how to paint, and Sophia knew they weren't born with the ability. Yes, the neighbor made a rather sexist statement when he expected the boys to maintain the house just because they were male, but this story about painting also makes me think about things we expect bright kids to be able to do just because they are intelligent.

We often expect smart young people to be organized, responsible, interested in school, and good at most academic subjects. We also expect them to be self-motivated, well-behaved, and to value the same things that we value. We think they should automatically know how to take notes, write papers, and prepare for exams. Although students may be smart, they are not born with expertise in all areas and we should not assume that they will have the skills necessary to demonstrate all of their capabilities.

Let's assume you have a child who is very bright. How might your expectations for that child shape her? Is it good to anticipate great things for your young person or can that cause too much pressure, leaving your student to feel that you only love her if she consistently performs at a high level? May your high expectations cause your young person to work hard to please you and then abandon all effort once he has left home?

How much should you expect from your gifted student, both academically and socially? What should you expect from yourself as a parent? How can you best understand some of the subtleties of giftedness? What should young people expect from themselves?

WORKING TO ONE'S POTENTIAL

Frequently one hears that *we must help children to reach their potential.* Working to one's potential is the expectation. Unfortunately, this is another term that is rather ambiguous in its meaning. How do we know exactly what anyone's potential is? How would we know when it was reached? Is it fair to ask a person to always do his best? What impact does asking one to reach her potential have on the actual output of a child?

Let's take this out of the realm of the gifted student for a moment. How does this fit in with your life? Do you know what your potential is? Have you achieved it? If you have, I assume you worked hard to get there. Would you want those around you to expect you to be at your peak performance at *all* times? Are there periods in your life when you have achieved great things and periods where you've just glided through the days or years? Would it cause a lot of pressure to strive to work to your potential all of the time? How do you know when it's too much pressure? What is the purpose of working to one's potential? Is a person a failure in life if he doesn't work as hard as possible all of the time?

Rather than expect a student to work to his potential, perhaps it would be a better to say we must help the child see the possibilities in life. The young person would then have to decide if he is willing to work toward those possibilities. The real effort needs to come from the internal drive of the individual.

What parents really want to know is how they can help their child achieve a high level of competence. They want the schools to provide an appropriate education so their student will reach an elevated level of proficiency.

What are your expectations of your child, your child's school, or yourself? What expectations are realistic and what expectations are asking too much?

WHAT DOES IT MEAN WHEN YOUR CHILD SAYS HE'S BORED?

We often think our children should be constantly and positively engaged. When a young person is bored, he knows he doesn't like what he's doing, but he doesn't know what to do about it. The phrase "I'm bored" sends waves of panic through some parents. When a child says he's bored at school, the immediate impulse is to do something to change the situation. But, what does it mean to be bored? Often we assume that it means the child is not being challenged and it is the job of adults to remedy that.

So, what does the term *bored* really mean? It has different meanings to different people and at different times. It could mean that the material a child is being taught is not challenging. Angela was struggling every day in class. She had been given the opportunity to enroll in Advanced Placement (AP) English, but she had chosen not to because she didn't want a lot of homework this year. Now she was suffering because of her decision. The class in which Angela was enrolled was simply not challenging enough to be interesting.

Boredom could mean that the student is not interested in the material being taught. David enjoyed reading, but only when he chose the subject matter. His teacher wanted the children to be exposed to and gain an appreciation for a variety of genres. So, David was required to read some books that were not of his choosing and he balked at this.

Boredom could mean that your young person is not in his comfort zone. After assessing the abilities of students, Joshua's teacher placed him in an advanced math group. The advanced material was a bit of a stretch for him. The previous year, Joshua had breezed through math and was feeling pretty cocky. This year, he struggled. He knew he felt uncomfortable and he interpreted that feeling as boredom.

It also could mean that your student would rather be with friends than doing schoolwork. Hailey was a very social individual. Her favorite part of the day was recess when she could be with her pals. Whenever there was an activity at school that she didn't want to do, she would daydream about being out on the playground. She told her parents she was bored.

Boredom might mean that your child would like to be home playing instead of at school. Let's look at the example of Caleb. Last week Caleb celebrated his birthday. His uncle gave him a great new computer game. Caleb had already made it to level four and was preoccupied with advancing to the next level. In class, his thoughts were consumed with the strategies he would try next. He definitely did not want to be in school, where he said he was bored. He wanted to be home playing that computer game.

As adults, we have to be careful not to jump to conclusions when children tell us they are bored. It would probably be helpful to ask your child to tell you what the word means to her. Ask probing questions, like "Can you tell me more about that?" or "How would you make things different if you could?" or "What would the perfect day look like?" Don't put words in the child's mouth such as, "Are you not learning anything new at school?"

Sometimes, we all get ourselves in situations that are terribly tedious or boring. Think of the times you accidentally got in the wrong line at the grocery store and you had to wait, seemingly forever, to check out. Or, think about the time your plane was delayed and you sat at the airport not knowing what was going to happen.

TABLE 4
Five Things Kids Can Do When Bored

Kids are frequently put in situations where they have little control. They're dragged along to the grocery store, have to wait while a sibling is at soccer practice, or they're in the car for a longer-than-predicted time. If they can keep a small backpack loaded with supplies, they always will have something to do. You also will help them learn to use their minds, no matter what the situation. Some supplies to keep in the backpack and tips for ways kids can use these supplies include the following:

1. Paper and pencil. Study the people around you. Notice their physical characteristics, how they're dressed, how they move their bodies, and so forth. Imagine their interests, jobs, and personality characteristics. Take notes about the people. The notes will make a great basis for a story to write later. You also can use the paper and pencil to draw or make lists of things you need to do or to remember, all the words you can think of that begin with a "Y," places you'd like to visit, and more.
2. Small book of word or math puzzles and a writing instrument.
3. MP3 player. Download music and audio or video podcasts in advance. These downloads are available online, even available for preschoolers—and many are free.
4. A book to read.
5. Handheld electronic game device.

Children need to understand that life isn't always fun, that everyone gets bored occasionally—or dislikes the task at hand—and that we all have to do things that we'd rather not. Help them to learn to mentally challenge themselves when caught in these situations. Table 4 includes a quick list of five things a child can do when he says he is bored.

When you get to Chapter 5, "The Value of Creativity," you will see that there are actually good things that can come from lack of engagement. It can lead to periods of creativity, giving the mind time to wander and the time necessary to put thoughts into action. However, if your child does have legitimate reasons for being bored in school, try approaching the problem from all angles. Talk with the teachers and/or administrators at the school about ways that your child might be more appropriately challenged. Because you cannot always control the school environment, also help your child to learn to challenge himself at school. How can he go more in depth with a subject or go in different directions with it? By moving toward these alternatives, you will help your child become responsible for her own learning, which is a very empowering skill.

So, when you hear your child say that she is bored, don't immediately panic and expect the worst. Investigate the underlying cause of the comment, determine its validity, and then act appropriately.

ORGANIZATION—THE FOUNDATION FOR PRODUCTIVITY

It is reasonable to expect parents to first teach kids organizational skills at home and then to have those skills reinforced in school.

Being asked to clean one's room or organize one's notebook is a daunting task for some young people and mastery may not come easily. One fun way for youngsters to learn how to do various jobs can be found at the Web site wikiHow (http://www.wikihow.com), where kids can search for ways to accomplish specific tasks. This might relieve parents from telling a son or daughter exactly how to do everything. For instance, there are articles on how to set goals, clean your room, organize your notebook, organize a bookshelf, organize your life, and be on time for school.

Yolanda had a heavy academic load, plus a number of out-of-school activities. She really needed to be able to plan ahead. To help her, she mounted a large erasable calendar on the backside of her closet door. On it she marked with a vis-à-vis pen each project, paper, and test that was coming up. Then, with her father's help, she worked backward, setting benchmark goals, reminding herself where she needed to be with her work in the coming days to be able to complete each assignment on time. It helped Yolanda a great deal to plan all of this out in advance. It also helped relieve a lot of stress for both Yolanda and her parents to see that she was on track.

There are lots of suggestions in adult books on organization that may be helpful for young people. The parents' sense of organization, as long as it's not compulsive, will go a long way in influencing children. Although students may appear to not care about organization, if they see the benefits for their parents of being organized day after day, year after year, eventually it tends to rub off.

It helps if organization cannot only be useful, but fun. Visit office supply stores and other stores that carry a variety of products designed to help with organization, such as color-coded envelopes, files, and pocket folders. The use of a day-timer or planner to record due dates is helpful. If you can afford it and your child is responsible, a handheld electronic device may be a good tool. Other ideas to help with organization include:

- using different color pens to record homework assignments in the planner;
- allowing enough time during transitions to record assignments and put materials away;
- marking assignments as they are finished to give your child a sense of accomplishment;
- placing materials to go to school or to take to a practice or lesson in a specific area near the door that your child exits (if this can be done the night before, it eliminates stress in the morning); and
- having adequate office supplies. It's difficult for a child to do homework if she can't find paper, pencils, scissors, tape, sticky notes, and so forth.

Expect your student to learn organization skills first at home from you, the parent, before you expect them to learn the skills at school.

EMOTIONAL INTELLIGENCE

Although we often place an emphasis on cognitive intelligence, emotional intelligence (EQ) also is critically important to personal development. *Emotional Intelligence: Why It Can Matter More Than IQ* (Goleman, 1997) is well worth reading. According to the author, intellect cannot work at its best without emotional intelligence, so it is best to find a balance between IQ and EQ. Goleman defines emotional intelligence in terms of self-awareness, management of one's emotions, self-motivation, empathy, and the art of relationships. Because he believes that emotional intelligence isn't fixed at birth, he outlines ways to develop these skills. He does not negate the importance of cognitive intelligence, but explains that to optimize that cognitive intelligence, a person must know how to work with others and to work with him- or herself.

By helping students work on their emotional intelligence, we help them see their roles in academic, personal, and social responsibilities. Each young person then discovers that:

- Good grades result from my efforts. If I want to learn it's ultimately up to me.
- It's up to me to make it happen. How I act matters.
- I care about what is good for all of us, not just for me.

By teaching these skills, we will help our young people to do well academically, use good judgment, conduct themselves with appropriate behavior, get along with people, bounce back from the bumps of life, and be good citizens. Parents should expect to help their students discover these values.

HOW MUCH SHOULD YOU HELP AND PROTECT YOUR CHILD?

Parenting is like walking a tightrope, constantly trying to balance the lives of all family members. We want our kids to be happy, and it is painful to watch them experience the bumps of life. We worry about their self-esteem and try to protect it. But beware—we cannot expect to protect them from all adversity. In fact, too much protection actually can be harmful.

Many parents fight to get their kids into more challenging academic classes because they know that challenge is healthy, yet these same caregivers often protect their youngsters from challenge in other aspects of their lives, such as dealing with uncomfortable situations, learning to work with people who have different ideas, earning money to purchase something they want, doing without a lot of material possessions, or learning to fill their own free time. We don't allow children to struggle in these situations because we are afraid it will damage their self-esteem. Some parents constantly hover over their children, trying to make the world just right for them. These well-meaning parents deprive their children of the confidence-building skills that come with struggle. Kids benefit when they are guided toward solving their own problems, not when adults try to solve the problems for them.

Qi was a junior in high school. She had many interests and abilities. When faced with choices for the next semester, she had a hard time making up her mind. How many honors courses should she take? Could she manage taking all advanced classes, plus be on the swim team and also continue her part-time job as a waitress at a local restaurant? Would there be any time left for friends or for a bit part in the upcoming community theater production? Qi's parents had very high expectations for her but also felt that certain interests should have priorities over others.

Rather than tell Qi what she would and would not be allowed to do, they sat down with her and helped guide her thinking. Which of her interests did she feel were the most important and why? What was a realistic amount of time each might take? What long- and short-term personal goals might each choice fulfill? How would she ultimately make her decision? After decisions are made, what back-up plans will be available should the situation become too stressful? By using such questioning techniques, Qi's parents did not try to rescue her by solving her problem or by telling her what to do; instead, they helped her to gain confidence in solving her own dilemmas.

Once Qi made her decision, her parents periodically asked if she felt the plan was working the way she had hoped it would. If not, how might she tweak it to make it work? Would she make the same choice again? Why or why not? Qi's parents expected Qi to learn to make good choices in life. To help her along this path they did not try to shelter her from the bumps in life; instead, they guided her to learn thinking skills that would help her to skillfully attack life's problems.

WHAT SHOULD YOU EXPECT TO TELL YOUR CHILD ABOUT HIS ABILITIES?

Parents should not expect their children to do well just because they're bright; instead, young people need to understand that it is through their efforts that they will do well. In fact, a growing body of evidence strongly suggests that labeling kids as smart actually may cause underperformance.

Carol Dweck, formerly from Columbia University and now at Stanford University, has spent the last 10 years studying the effect of praise on students in New York schools (Dweck, 2007). She found that, when given a choice, students who were praised for their intelligence chose easier work so that they could still look smart. They didn't want to risk making mistakes. Countering this, 90% of the children who were praised for their effort instead of their intelligence chose harder work.

The students in Dweck's (2007) study were presented with very difficult tasks. Dweck found that those who had been praised for effort got very involved and were willing to try all of the puzzles they had been given, many remarking that "This was my favorite test." Those who had been praised for their intelligence had a different reaction—they found the test to be very stressful. Dweck concluded that emphasizing effort gives a child something he or she can control.

In follow-up interviews, it was found that those who thought that innate intelligence was the most important ingredient of success felt that they did not need to put out effort. Dweck (2007) found that this effect of praise held true for students of every socioeconomic class, and was especially true of the very brightest girls.

To be effective, researchers also have found that praise needs to be both sincere and specific (i.e., I like how you keep trying, you listened well to instructions, you concentrated for a long time without taking a break, or your free throws during the basketball game were very good). When people are given general praise like "You did a good job," they may not understand exactly what they did right. They also may feel the praise is not genuine.

Because young people inevitably will fail at times, they must have strategies for dealing with that failure. When a parent ignores a child's failures and insists that the young person will do better the next time, the child may come to believe that failure is so terrible that the family can't acknowledge its existence. A youngster deprived of the opportunity to discuss mistakes can't learn from them. Dweck (2007) wants students to believe that the way to bounce back from failure is to work harder. By developing this trait of persistence, students are able to sustain motivation through long periods of delayed gratification. If one is rewarded too much, she will learn to quit when those rewards disappear.

Parents need to expect their children to work hard, to fail at times, and to learn from their mistakes.

FEELING VALUED

Parents should expect to value each of their children. For example, Jessica and Rachael were 2 years apart in age. They each clamored for their parents' attention. Being sensitive to this, the parents made every effort to praise the girls individually for their strengths. They did not want the siblings to feel that they were in competition with one another, but that each girl was valued for her own traits.

"Jessica," her mother would say, "you work so hard at your artwork. I love to see your finished products."

"Rachael," her father would voice, "you are so nice to your friends. I know how much they must appreciate you."

Jessica and Rachael's parents were careful never to say things like "I wish you would work as hard at school as your sister," or "Why can't you be more like . . . ?"

Bring to the attention of each of your children his strengths, whether they are academic strengths, personality traits, thinking abilities, or artistic talents. It is likely that each youngster will have different strengths, and it's actually quite exciting that they are different. Although your daughter may be very good at math, your son may be a great athlete. Although your son may keep his room very tidy, your daughter may love to sing and dance.

CONCLUSION

Being labeled as gifted can be a mixed bag. The intent of identifying children as gifted or talented is to help teachers and parents be aware of academic and affective needs they might have. One of the negative aspects of labeling kids is that sometimes unrealistic expectations are placed upon them, so we must guard against that. When we identify children (either formally or informally) as able learners, it is helpful to specify their areas of strength. We cannot assume that because they are bright in one domain that they are exceptionally intelligent in all areas. In fact, a child may have extraordinary capabilities in one area and be below average in another.

Although it is important to have expectations for gifted children, it also is important to remember that the ultimate responsibility for raising and educating a young person lies with the parents, not with someone else.

4

PARENTAL RESPONSIBILITIES

SOMETIMES, we become frustrated because neighborhood schools do not meet the needs of bright kids. Parents have options—but one option that is not acceptable is to continue to protest a child's poor education without acting positively. To be effective, parents of bright children have the responsibility to learn as much as they can about gifted education, to work with schools and districts in constructive ways, and to offer enrichment and other learning opportunities outside of school.

EDUCATE YOURSELF

First and foremost, educate yourself. Read everything you can about giftedness and gifted education, including books, magazines, journals, and appropriate Web sites. (See the resources section at the end of this book for good starting places in addition to the suggestions offered in the various chapters.) Join and become active in state and local gifted associations and other support organizations for gifted education. Attend national, state, and local gifted conferences.

Without enough background information about the needs and possibilities for gifted students, it will be difficult for you to make the best choices for your children and also to speak with credibility when working with teachers and administrators. Know that there are not only many different definitions of the term *gifted*, but also many different philosophies about ways to work with bright kids. You will find that many of the ideas in the resources at the end of this book do not agree with one another and that's okay. What is important for you to know is that there are choices and no one right way to understand or work with smart young people.

WORK WITH SCHOOLS AND DISTRICTS IN CONSTRUCTIVE WAYS

Once you have educated yourself about gifted education and feel that you want to relate information to teachers or request that educational modifications be made for your child, approach your young person's teacher. Work with your school and district in a positive, helpful manner. Be assertive, but not aggressive. Assertive parents present positive, educated alternatives and suggestions that build bridges. Aggressive parents cause educators to build walls of defense and create alienation.

Communicating With Schools: A Positive Approach

One Colorado school district (Cherry Creek Schools, n.d.) has developed specific suggestions for parents wishing to support their gifted child's education. Some tips for working effectively with schools and teachers include:

- Request a convenient time to speak with your child's teacher.
- Provide your questions and concerns in writing before meeting the teacher.
- Be willing to compromise and collaborate on behalf of the student's needs.
- Provide a home perspective to your child's teacher on a regular basis.
- Keep a file of communications, learning plans, and testing data on your child throughout his or her K–12 years.
- Provide both positive and negative feedback for changes in your child's learning plan, school assignments, and learning activities.
- Always give your child's teacher a second chance to discuss educational issues about your child.
- Determine reasonable timelines and methods for communicating with your child's teacher.
- Do not expect your child to provide complete or accurate descriptions of school-day experiences. Communicate directly with your child's teachers if you have questions about what is happening in the classroom.
- Celebrate excellence both for your child and for those who teach your child.

There are many approaches schools use to try to meet the educational needs of gifted students. Some schools actually have no plan; others have a one-size-fits-all plan for able students; still others have a plan that increases services according to the level of giftedness for each student. Strategies may include one or more of the following:

- *Cluster grouping*—identified gifted students at a grade level are assigned to one classroom with a teacher who has special training in how to teach gifted students. Curriculum modifications are made for this group. Other students in their assigned class are of mixed ability. By using this strategy, gifted students are able to interact with their intellectual, as well as age, peers.

- *Curriculum compacting*—students who demonstrate they have mastered course content, or can master course content more quickly, can opt out of some of the regular classroom work. They "buy time" to study material that they find more challenging and interesting.

- *Acceleration*—moving to more advanced material. This may be accomplished by skipping a grade, moving to a higher grade for just one or two subjects, or working at a higher level while staying with one's age peers.

- *Differentiation*—adjustment of the curriculum, based on a student's academic need and ability. This adjustment may take place by modifying the content of the curriculum, how the curriculum is delivered, and/or the final product(s) expected from the student.

- *Pull-out classes*—a specialist takes a group of students outside the regular classroom for instruction. This is done during the school day.
- *Enrichment programs and projects*—content is extended beyond the regular curriculum. These classes or events may take place before or after school or during school hours.
- *Affective support*—help with social and emotional needs either for individuals or in groups.
- *Advanced Placement (AP) classes*—advanced courses with a designated curriculum covering material either in content areas or elective areas. If students receive certain scores on final tests, they may enter college with credit for those classes.
- *Independent study*—projects that are designed for a student based on a special interest or to allow the student to investigate a topic in depth or on his own.
- *Honors classes*—advanced versions of classes offered to the regular school population.
- *International Baccalaureate (IB)*—a program only offered at schools that have applied and been approved by the international organization. It is a rigorous series of coursework based on a global philosophy. Although it most often is found at the high school level, it is available for students from ages 3–19.
- *Magnet school*—schools that draw on the population of the entire district, rather than the local neighborhood. There usually are entrance requirements. As the

popularity of these schools grow, there are more and more of these specialty schools that cater to the needs or interests of the high-ability population.

- *Special GT seminars/classes*—such classes are frequently held during vacation breaks and focus on specialty areas of academics or special interests.

If you have a child who is of high ability, that student should experience curriculum that has more rigor and depth than the regular grade-level curriculum. Although you should look out for the academic interests of your child, you also need to recognize when teachers are doing their best for all students.

For more than a decade, Cynthia worked as a gifted and talented resource teacher in a public school that had an excellent academic record and was known for working with very bright kids. Although it wasn't a specialized school, a high number of students were identified as gifted using a combination of test scores, higher level thinking skills, and teacher/parent recommendations. Frequently, Cynthia had very concerned parents call her. They wanted to talk about their sons and daughters and questioned many aspects of their students' education. Cynthia listened to the parents talk as they voiced their thoughts and concerns, and then she asked the question, "Do you feel that your child's needs are being met?" Inevitably their answers were, "Well, yes, but I just want to make certain that everything is being done for my child that should be done." It was easy for Cynthia to address this question because she knew the high quality of education that took place at this particular school.

Teachers really worked to play into the strengths of each child and challenge every student. This was an exceptional school.

The parents at this school wanted to talk because they felt a sense of responsibility. In addition to having concerns about academics, they often felt that they only had one shot at successful parenting. They wanted to understand the best way to accomplish this. They wanted to assure themselves that they were doing everything they could.

PROVIDE ENRICHMENT AND OTHER LEARNING OPPORTUNITIES OUTSIDE OF SCHOOL

When my kids were young, the many interest-based classes available today did not exist. I worked hard to find everything that was offered in our city and then carefully coordinated schedules in the summer to present the kids with as many choices as possible. The spring before the boys entered the third and fifth grades, we moved to a rural area. Facing the drive every day to get them to the various courses felt overwhelming to me. So, I sat my two boys down and told them they wouldn't be able to take classes that upcoming summer. To my surprise, one of them said, "You mean we don't have to go all of those classes?" Here I thought I had been providing them with something they wanted to do, and I finally realized that they didn't know they had a choice.

That summer was a happy one for all of us. I didn't have to do so much driving and the kids were able to explore their new surroundings, get to meet others in the neighborhood, and be left to their own creative devices.

Although enrichment offerings are very important to children, it also is important to remember to have balance in the life of the family. As you read through the many possibilities suggested in this chapter, remember that this is a menu from which to choose. No one should expect to do it all.

Enrichment offers exposure to opportunities beyond the traditional curriculum and shows young people the possibilities of life. Although enrichment can take place during school time, it also may take place before or after school, on weekends, or during vacations. The possibilities are limitless. Consider children's classes that are offered by individual instructors, private agencies, symphony organizations, theater groups, museums, zoos, and local colleges and universities. Expose your child to experiences such as travel, plays, and live music.

Below, I have listed opportunities based on general categories. Some are expensive, while others cost little or nothing. Remember, this is only the tip of the iceberg of possibilities.

Games, Toys, and Puzzles

Games and puzzles are not only a relatively inexpensive way to offer enrichment, they also are excellent family activities. When chosen carefully, they build higher level thinking and behavioral skills, including concentration, patience, perseverance, analysis, logic, and problem solving. There are the old classic games like Chess and Tri-ominos®; puzzles such as crossword puzzles, jigsaw puzzles, and Sudoku; and computer and video games.

On special occasions, adults scramble to find presents for gifted children that will be fun, help them to grow intellectually, and have lasting value. If chosen appropriately, board games, card games, construction toys, books, puzzles, and computer software serve these needs in a most satisfying way. Many of these are self-limiting and hold a child's interest for only a short time. Others can have a real impact on a person's life. Consider items that require higher level thinking and reasoning, encourage creative thinking, teach new facts or ideas, and can be used over and over again.

Quality toys and activities usually require seeing patterns, making plans, searching combinations, judging alternative moves, and learning from experience. A few places to view lists of quality toys and activities include:

- The Davidson Institute (Resources Page)—http://www. gt-cybersource.org
- Hoagies' Gifted Education Page: Gifts for the Gifted— http://www.hoagiesgifted.org/shopping_guide.htm
- Mindware—http://www.mindwareonline.com/ MWESTORE/Home/HomePage.aspx?
- Winners of the Mensa Select® Distinction (Marketplace Page) —http://www.us.mensa.org

Several software companies also provide excellent choices for games for children, including the following:

- Knowledge Adventure—http://www.knowledgeadventure.com

  Some highlights from this company are Math Blaster, Jumpstart series, and Dr. Brain series.
- The Learning Company—http://www.learningcompany.com

  Recommended titles include Sammy's Science House, The Oregon Trail, the Carmen Sandiego series, and Zoombini's Logical Journey.
- Scholastic Corporation (which now also owns Tom Snyder Productions)—http://store.scholastic.com or http://www.tomsnyder.com

  Titles include I Spy series, MaxData, Tesselation Exploration, and Operation Frog Deluxe.

Remember that your children—no matter their ages—will enjoy playing games and solving puzzles with you. Much of the learning experience comes from discussing the various possible strategies used—what works, what doesn't work, and why. Scrabble® has always been one of our big family games. We started playing together when the kids were just learning to spell and we all still play as adults. It helps to talk out loud about strategies used and why a player chose to put a word down in a particular place or why he decided to save certain letters for a better opportunity.

When choosing a game, toy, or puzzle, consider not only the child's abilities but also his interests. For example, Thiago Olson's interest in science began with mixing things together in the kitchen (his mother thought he would be a cook), a simple chemistry set, and the ability to meet other science enthusiasts on the Internet. His friends called the teenager "the mad scientist." In the basement of his parents' home, Thiago spent more than 2 years and 1,000 hours to research and build a machine that, on a small scale, creates nuclear fusion. He was 15. Because he was in cross-country and track, he couldn't work on the project constantly, so it was more of a weekend project. That chemistry set that Thiago received early on certainly helped him to develop his love of science, leading to a future scientific project.

We can provide a game, toy, or puzzle that supports a child's interests, or we can give one that may introduce the young person to something new. I surveyed family members and friends by posing the question: "What are your memories of your best holiday presents—ones that really got you interested in something that you continued to pursue?" The following is a synthesis of responses:

- Computer—This was used to play games, learn simple programming, and figure out how computers work—this person went on to a profession in computers. He now builds and maintains computer systems for individuals, companies, and governments.
- Video camera—This inexpensive camera was used to make very creative movies. The individual learned movie editing skills and gained a lot of positive recognition from friends for her creativity. In the end, it encouraged creativity in all aspects of her life.

- A basic stereo—Receiving this stereo as a teenager conveyed that his parents supported his love of music. He now has a career in the radio industry.
- Erector set—This mechanical building set taught one child principals of mechanics and helped him to develop manual skills. Eventually this person became an orthopedic surgeon.
- Diary with a lock and key and lots of stationery and pencils and pens—These tools helped this person learn to love to write. As a teenager, she had pen pals all over the world, so she also learned a lot about geography and different cultures. She eventually became a writer and editor.
- A simple chemistry set with a rocket that could be launched with vinegar and soda, and also chemicals and directions for making invisible ink, fake blood, and other mixtures—The parents of this child did not have much money and it was a sacrifice for them to purchase the kit. The child was sensitive to this and appreciated it. This person went on to become a psychologist and high school counselor—always sensitive to the needs of others.
- An adult received a copy of the book *Writer's Market*, which is the bible for those wanting to publish their writing—It was a personal signal that she should take her writing seriously and she has since published numerous articles and two books.
- Twenty-gallon fish tank—Receiving this gift turned into a lifelong hobby of the study of fish and underwater ecosystems.

Hopefully, when choosing toys, games, and puzzles, you will consider ones that will help your young person develop a skill and encourage creativity. One never knows how this might translate into a lifelong endeavor.

Support Interests and Hobbies

If your child shows an interest, support it in every way possible, even if it isn't your personal interest. You never know where this interest might lead.

Armando wanted to watch the same videos over and over and over again. Sometimes, he would watch the same movie 20 or 25 times. His parents had read that too much television is a bad thing for children. Surely this also was true of videos, they thought. Although his mom and dad tried to encourage Armando to do other things, every time they turned their backs, he was back watching his movies. What his parents didn't understand was what Armando was learning from this interest. By the time he was in high school, Armando began verbalizing his thoughts about movies. After the family would watch a movie together, he would express his opinions and was very detailed about the effect of certain lighting techniques, placement of objects on the screen, and key lines that were cited. By the time he was in college, he was writing film reviews for the local newspaper. He had developed an incredible talent for observing the nuances of film.

Jason was passionate about astronomy. He began asking questions about space after seeing a program on television about our solar system. He read every book he could from the local library on the subject and asked his dad to help him find more television programs about the universe. Soon Jason learned how to locate information on the Internet. His father described how he supported his son's interest by introducing him to others who shared the same passion. They visited a planetarium to see special presentations and attended meetings of the local astronomical association. Although neither of Jason's parents had special knowledge in the area of astronomy or a strong interest in it, they were able to support their son by providing a community of practitioners in the field.

As Jake was growing up, home was such a fun place to be. There was always something to do. Jake was interested in the weather, building models, HO gauge trains, beekeeping, and sailing, among other things. He kept a small ringed notebook and every day he cut the weather map out of the paper and pasted it in. Using the thermometers and barometers at the house, he recorded the high and low temperatures and the air pressure. He made his own predictions of the short- and long-term forecasts and also noted whether he had been correct on the previous day.

Model airplanes that Jake built hung from the ceiling in his bedroom and the dresser was covered with ships he had assembled. While in elementary school, Jake saved his money from doing odd jobs for neighbors and family to start buying model trains. In the basement, he created a setup of plywood that rested on wooden horses. On this platform he created the layout of a miniature town and countryside. He built every house, created every tree and road, and constructed every bridge. When he was in junior high school, Jake started beekeeping and eventually had four hives. He would harvest the honey and sell it to friends and family. He had an arrangement with the school principal to let him out of school whenever a swarm left a hive so he could retrieve it. Jake first experimented with sailing by fastening a rig on an old aluminum rowboat. When he was a preteen, he built a two-man sailboat from scratch in the family's garage.

The kids in Jake's family all had rocks, shells, and mounted insects that they collected. Everyone learned how to play at least one instrument. The kids had some hobbies that required a financial investment, but they also had many hobbies that didn't cost a cent. The children were very fortunate because their parents encouraged them to explore many interests. The parents felt as long as the kids were learning new things, they were having valuable experiences.

A hobby is a specialized pursuit (e.g., stamp collecting, painting, dancing) that is outside the child's regular school work and that she finds particularly interesting and enjoys doing as a source of leisure-time relaxation. Broadly, it is any favorite pursuit or interest. Although hobbies benefit all kids, gifted children can gain enormously from them. Hobbies broaden the interests of children, inspire new ways of thinking, release stress, and enhance competence. They also encourage tenacity, organization, and creative thinking.

Summer Experiences

Summer experiences come in all shapes, sizes, and interests. Although opportunities exist for elementary school children, the variety and specialties really increase for students in middle and high school. These opportunities may include volunteering, travel to another country, advanced academic work, fine arts, leadership experiences, internships, or exposure to a new field of possible interest. There are day camps and overnight camps. You and your child need to decide the purpose of enrolling, ask a lot of questions, and be sure to get references.

PARENT RESOURCES: SUMMER OPPORTUNITIES

Some places where you can find more information on summer opportunities include:

- American Camp Association—http://www.acacamps.org This Web site has a large, searchable database.
- Berger, S. L. (2008). *The ultimate guide to summer opportunities for teens*. Waco, TX: Prufrock Press.

    Information is listed by state; academic field; fine, performing, and visual arts; international travel; internships; and leadership,
- Cogito, through Johns Hopkins University—http://www.cogito.org

    Click on "Summer Programs." Here you will find an incredible list of science and math possibilities.
- Davidson Institute's GT-CyberSource—http://www.gt-cybersource.org

    Search "Summer Programs" under "Resources" for a long list of possibilities.
- Hoagies' Gifted Education Page: Summer and Saturday Programs—http://www.hoagiesgifted.org/summer.htm

    This has a list of both national and international programs to consider.

- Institute for Educational Advancement (IEA Gifted Resource Center)—http://www.educationaladvancement.org

  Click on "Programs." Provided here is an extensive searchable database by type of program, grade/age level, state, commuter/residential, and more.
- NAGC Resource Directory—http://www.nagc.org/resourcedirectory.aspx

  This site lists all types of services for students, including summer camps and services according to academic specialty, outdoor education, the arts, and technology.

You also will find information about specific summer opportunities within other chapters in this book. For instance, many summer programs are part of talent search opportunities for talented children.

COLLEGE PLANNING

To be effective, college planning needs to start much earlier than most families realize. Sandra Berger (2006), a college-planning expert, recommends that gifted students start planning for and thinking about college as early as seventh grade. Don't worry if you're uncertain about where or when to begin helping your child with college planning. Many resources exist to aid parents on this topic.

Imagine magazine (http://cty.jhu.edu/imagine), published by Johns Hopkins University Center for Talented Youth, is a great aid. I recommend beginning a subscription while your student is in seventh or eighth grade. Each issue explores topics ranging from mathematics, to writing, to computer science. Included are articles about summer programs and extracurricular activities across the country, as well as advice on planning for college, student reviews of selective colleges, and profiles of fascinating careers. Each issue is devoted to a broad focus topic (e.g., medicine, mathematics, going green) showcasing activities that students can do now to pursue that interest, as well as career opportunities in the field.

College Planning for Gifted Students: Choosing and Getting Into the Right College (Berger, 2006), is a comprehensive guide for motivated students. It includes sections on gifted students with disabilities and homeschoolers. The author walks college-hopefuls through every step, from making an educational plan in seventh grade, to writing a successful essay, asking for letters of recommendation, and making the final choice.

Families who feel they do not have financial resources to send their gifted kids on to school—especially a highly selective school—should not be discouraged. In the not so distant past, spots in elite schools in the United States were reserved only for the wealthy. Today, it is possible for those without financial resources to get the best education at the best schools. To accomplish this, though, students need to work hard.

There actually seems to be a competition now among some of the elite schools of higher learning to recruit students from lower socioeconomic statuses. At some of these schools, if the family earns less than $60,000 a year, the students pay no tuition. This is all part of a growing national movement to combat the rapidly rising cost of higher education and to ensure that elite universities don't shut out all but the wealthiest students. In addition, students are eligible to apply for federal financial aid, including grants, scholarships, and loans, by completing a FAFSA form (found at http://www.fafsa.ed.gov). Submitting the form is free and open to any college-bound student. Keep in mind that your child will not be able to receive financial aid if you do not complete the form. So, realize that capable students who set high academic goals and work hard should not allow their minds to close to the possibility of an excellent college education.

CONCLUSION

You ultimately are responsible for the education of your bright children. To do an effective job, you must learn as much as you can about gifted education, work with schools and districts in constructive ways, and offer enrichment and other learning opportunities outside of school.

5

THE VALUE OF CREATIVITY

Lots of people are "book smart," but it is the individual who is creative within his field who makes a real difference in the world.

Who are the people who bring us great books or fine art or architecture or innovative computer programs? Who are the people who find medical cures or bring about social change? They are individuals who "think outside the box." They are those who are willing to be adventuresome and take risks with their thinking. They are some of our most creative people.

Creativity is important in both the arts and in academics. Although kids need a good academic education, beginning with the basics, it is through the development of imagination and innovation that they are able to truly demonstrate their intellect.

When making conference presentations on creativity, I usually ask adult participants to raise their hands if they feel they are creative. I am always surprised at how few hands shoot up in the air. Upon further exploration, it often is revealed that people don't give themselves permission to be creative. In their minds, they have a lot of "rules" that discourage creativity. During our time together, we practice removing some of those barriers and participants often leave the room with a newfound freedom to be creative.

Some people seem to be born creative and others find it an arduous task. Whether one is born with this skill or not, the ability to improve one's imagination can be enhanced. That's what we work on in these adult sessions and that's what we need to work on with kids at home and at school.

Some tips for encouraging creativity at home include:

- Tolerate uncertainty. Do not expect answers immediately. Give your child time to think. Have you ever replied to a question right away and then wished you had given a different answer? Postponing your reply allows time for better answers.
- Do not require that everything be tidy all of the time. Some projects dictate a bit of temporary chaos—especially building and science projects.
- Choose play materials carefully. Minimal materials allow kids to create their own recreation. Supply toys and projects that encourage imagination rather than stifle it. (See Chapter 4 for suggestions.) Provide tools that have the broadest range of possibilities, such as blank paper rather than a coloring book.
- View mistakes as positive learning tools, recognizing that taking mental risks eventually can lead to great creations.

THE AHA! EXPERIENCE

Think about the times when you get your best ideas. For many adults, the answers are when washing the dishes, driving, taking a shower, or doing any mundane task that doesn't require concentration. Usually, real creativity is a three-step process:

- First, one is presented with a problem: How can I solve this predicament at work? Where shall we go on vacation? Why is this appliance not working?
- Next, there needs to be time for that problem to incubate in one's mind. It helps to place the problem in one's subconscious for a while and just let it sit there.
- Finally, there is an "aha" experience where a solution to the problem comes to mind. The solution often occurs suddenly to a person when he is not consciously thinking about it. Some people even awake in the middle of the night with such an experience.

You may have noticed that when you schedule less in your life and move at a slower pace, you often are more productive and definitely more creative. That slower pace allows time for the necessary building blocks of life: adequate sleep, healthy diet, and quality exercise. When you are physically and mentally prepared to handle tasks, you have more time to organize your life. You also have time for your mind to wander. The tendency in society is to fill every minute of our lives. When we do that, we may feel that we're accomplishing a lot, but the accomplishments we have may not be very creative.

Understanding the process of creativity will help you see how it can be improved. If we rush to figure out how to best solve a problem, we may overlook some of the best choices. In today's age of instant gratification, we want instant answers. How many times have you been asked to do something or attend an event and right away you answered affirmatively only to later regret your answer? Perhaps it would be better to say, "Let me think about that," or "I'll have to get back to you on that."

Moving this concept of delaying response to a child's realm, let's assume your child wants to display his rock collection. Wanting to help your young person problem solve and delay an immediate response, you may ask, "What are all of the different ways you can think of to organize the rocks?" (i.e., according to size, shape, color, hardness); "What are choices of ways they might be displayed?" (i.e., in a box, on a shelf, with a colorful backdrop); "What are some choices of locations where they could be displayed?"; and "Is there anything you could add to the display to make it more attractive/interesting?" Encouraging immediate answers eliminates the thoughtfulness that comes with time to think.

LESS IS MORE

You don't have to spend money on toys and entertainment to encourage creativity in very young children. All you need to do is look around the house and think about different ways of using the things you already have. With minimal materials, young people will open up their minds to imagination.

For instance, you may use everyday items in new ways:

- Sheets and blankets draped across furniture make great playhouses. This may mean rearranging the furniture (temporary chaos). Add some stuffed animals and a whole fantasy world can be constructed. Take small figures outside and let young children create a fantasy world in the garden.

- Keep a box of unused or discarded hats, costume jewelry, shoes, and clothing to be used to play dress-up. Make sure a full-length mirror is available so kids can see how they look. An old slip may suddenly become the gown of a princess, especially when combined with a necklace and a feathery boa. Garage sales and thrift shops also are inexpensive places to buy items for the dress-up box.

- Plastic bottles of various sizes that have been emptied and washed out make great bathtub toys that float or are used as pouring vessels. A plastic bowl may become a boat. All can be stored under the sink in a tote box.

- Recycle your clean Styrofoam meat trays, tin foil, and bubble wrap. Save all kinds of odds and ends of ribbon, string, yarn, sewing scraps, colorful paper, catalogs, and so forth. Whenever you're going to throw something out, look at it and think if your child might use it in a creative way. Keep the items in a special area for the kids to use on a rainy day. Coupled with scissors, markers, and glue, youngsters can construct artwork and inventions.

- When Halloween rolls around, don't go out and buy costumes; instead, let your kids choose who or what they want to be and decide together how the costume can be made. What everyday materials can be used in a new way? For example, Samantha wanted to be a spider for Halloween. To make the costume, she took a large balloon and covered it with papier mâché, then, with the help of her dad, cut an opening so she could slip it over her head and upper body. Next, her dad cut holes for the eyes. They took metal coat hangers, cut and bent them into the shape of the spider's legs, and covered them with wrappings of cloth. Once the costume was assembled, they spray painted it black.

When encouraged, most young people are capable of creating elaborate fantasy worlds. One time Paige and Justin decided they were birds. Another time they decided they were frogs. With each fantasy, they created songs, rhymes, ways that they moved their bodies, games they played, and secret languages. It would have been easy for their mother to discourage this, especially when they decided that birds only eat with their beaks. After all, that did not foster good manners at the dinner table. However, their mother knew the fantasy wouldn't last forever, so she let them pretend. They were developing their creativity and having a lot of fun with it.

Ways in which kids are creative change as they get older. They may be innovative in the ways they approach school projects, do chores at home, solve math problems, or just have fun. At this age, the same adage "Less is more" is still true.

Isabella, Daniel, and Emma are examples of students whose creativity incorporated new mediums as they got older. When Isabella was in middle school, her parents allowed her to use the family video camera. She produced novel videos that were driven by themes or stories she developed and included friends and family members. Among some of her videos were:

- "Cooking With Isabella," an amusing combination of a television food program, slapstick comedy, and interviews.
- "What to Do on a Snowy Day," modeled on a news format and using everyday items around the house in unusual ways.
- "Gerbils at Work," using trick photography to give the household pets paying jobs in the "real world."

Daniel enjoyed computers. He made a password protected, interactive Web site to share with extended family members around the country. It included a calendar of birthdays and anniversaries, a family tree and history, and a place where family stories could be recorded.

Emma became interested in Rube Goldberg, a cartoonist who drew complex devices that perform simple tasks in indirect, convoluted ways. Taking off on Goldberg's ideas, Emma created some of her own inventions, including complicated ways to do each of the household chores assigned to her.

ELEMENTS OF CREATIVITY

Elements of creativity include fluency, flexibility, originality, and elaboration. Each of these elements can be practiced and improved upon through fun family activities.

Fluency: Let the Ideas Flow

Fluency is the generation of lots of ideas, plans, or products. If you can generate many different ideas, you will have a greater chance of finding a good one. Let's say you want to change the furniture arrangement in your living room. You could go with the first arrangement that comes to your mind, or you could try to figure out all of the possible arrangements and then think about the pros and cons of each.

You can practice fluency at home with your kids with any type of problem solving. What can you do with your free time? Where should we go on vacation? How can you solve the conflict with your brother? What topic will you choose for your report at school?

To generate many possible solutions to these problems, brainstorm ideas together. To be effective, adhere to the following brainstorming guidelines:

1. No criticism is allowed. Defer any judgment until a large number of alternatives have been produced. (If you judge too quickly, you risk shutting people down.)

2. Freewheeling is urged. The wilder the ideas, the better. (From those crazy ideas just might come some very sensible ones.)

3. Quantity is desired. Include the small, obvious alternatives, as well as the wild, unusual, and clever ones. (The more ideas a person can generate, the greater the chances that one of those ideas will be a good one.)

4. Combine listed items or take an idea and modify it to produce even more possibilities. (Often young children will complain: "He stole my idea." But, it's a compliment to take someone else's idea and change it slightly or expand upon it.)

The following activities can help your kids develop fluent thinking:

1. Choose a common word. See how many different synonyms you can find for that word.

2. How many aspects are similar/different between these two books?

3. How many ways did WWII affect the culture of the U.S.?

4. List as many equations as you can where the answer is 6 ($3 + 3$, 2×3, $26 - 20$, and so on).

5. Name as many kinds of penguins as you can and their natural habitats.

While fluent thinkers try to come up with many ideas, flexible thinkers look for great variety.

Flexibility: Bending Minds

Think of trees in a violent storm. The older trees often are large and rigid. Sometimes their size and strength help them to withstand the gale-force winds, but sometimes that same rigidity causes them to snap. The younger, smaller trees are very flexible. Their coping mechanism for survival is to bend with the wind. This bending enables them to be resilient, to withstand great adversity. This also is true with people. At some time during one's lifespan, everyone has to endure difficult times. Being flexible during these difficult times can help a person be resilient—to bounce back more quickly—to see that there are choices and that there are different ways to look at problems and solutions—to be creative.

The flexible, creative mind seeks varied answers or solutions. Flexible thinkers go beyond the bounds of orthodox thinking as they seek and consider alternatives others fail to note. Although they use rules as guidelines, these rules are not treated as straight-jackets that curb thinking.

Flexibility requires that people escape from ruts and try new things. These thinkers are able to shift gears easily. They look for new ideas everywhere. They are not afraid of change.

The following activities can help your kids develop flexible thinking:

1. List as many unusual family vacations as possible. The wilder and wackier the better (e.g., trip to the moon, vacation in a cave or underwater sea area, or visit different amusement parks and ride all of the roller coasters).

2. What are all of the ways you could make it fun to clean your room or do other chores (e.g., have a race with a timer, give yourself a small reward every half hour, or pretend you are preparing for the visit of a queen)?

3. Discuss the way one family member's actions might be interpreted by other members of the household. (Kids being noisy at bedtime might be seen as fun for the children, but disturbing for the parents. Mom or dad telling kids to go out and play might feel like a healthy suggestion for the parents, but rejection for the youngsters. Kids not wanting to eat certain foods may feel like an exertion of choice for the children, but rudeness to the cook.) Try to explore these options in a nonjudgmental manner. You may find the different interpretations enlightening.

4. Practice switching activities quickly and efficiently (e.g., school, to home, to piano lessons, to soccer practice, to dinner, to homework, to bedtime).

5. Share fairy tales, history, biographies, or political accounts that have been written from different points of view.

6. When trying to resolve a conflict between friends or siblings, have each young person analyze the disagreement from the other person's point of view.

7. Give students a list of 50 famous inventors (or any other group of people, animals, objects, etc.). How many ways can they categorize this group? (Examples for inventors: male/female, century in which the inventor lived, types

of inventions, native countries, last names that begin with the same letter.)

While flexible thinkers look for variety, original thinkers try to come up with unique ideas.

Originality: Innovation at Its Best

Hanna stood in front of the mirror in her room, draped in the sheet from her bed. Last night she wore the sheet as a Roman dress. Tonight she adorned herself as the princess from a fantasy book she was reading. Her mother came in to say goodnight. "Ah," her mom sighed, knowing the bed would need to be remade yet again. Although this was a nuisance, Hanna's mother also understood that Hanna had a very original way of looking at things.

One father often heard the following comment about his two grown boys: "They are both so creative and so funny. How did they get to be that way?" The people who made these comments were correct; Shawn and Darin were very creative. Having a good sense of humor was probably part of that creativity. When they became adults, their innovation demonstrated itself in their approach to their jobs, solutions to personal problems, and the way they spent their spare time. More often than not, they greeted life in a very upbeat fashion.

Originality is the ability to generate unique, clever, and unusual responses to prompts or tasks. Original thinkers perceive and respond to the world in fresh, new ways. Originality is characterized by novelty.

When your kids were very young, I'm sure you did everything possible to child-proof your house. You were probably then shocked to find out that you hadn't done a complete job, because your young person found a way to use something in a way that you had never anticipated. She was thinking originally.

In another example, it never occurred to one mother that her child would "mail" anything he could find through the slots in the louvered cabinets. She discovered this one day when she was not able to find an important piece of paper she had laid on the table.

Young children need to be watched constantly because they find dangerous ways to use common objects like household cleaning products and electricity. They want to use these in creative ways, but often they do not understand the danger inherent in using such items. They are thinking originally. There are also ways to be original that are not so dangerous. When he was in ninth grade, Alex decided to hand out Halloween treats in a unique manner. With some old scrap lumber, he fashioned a casket. Then he borrowed a tuxedo from a neighbor and projected spooky music from the windows of the house. Alex set the casket at the end of the walk next to the street and, wearing the tuxedo, got in, taking the Halloween candy with him. He had drilled a peephole in the side of the casket so he could see the trick-or-treaters as they approached. As the children drew near, he slowly lifted the lid of the casket and gradually sat up and stared at them. The youngsters needed to come right up to the casket to get their candy. It certainly was an original way of delivering the treats.

Activities that encourage and develop a child's originality include the following:

1. Have children create costumes for one another using only newspapers and toothpicks.
2. Collect good jokes and cartoons. Make a scrapbook.
3. Play with words in regular conversations. Use puns, spoonerisms, alliteration, and other word plays.
4. Study inventors and inventions together. How did the inventors view problems in unusual ways, enabling them to create ingenious solutions?
5. Take a concrete object, such as a table, and have students imagine what it looks like from the point of view of an insect (might only see what is immediately in front of its eyes), a baby (might be lying on the floor and only see the underneath part of the table), an adult (possibly looking sideways or down on the object), and an elephant (may seem very small).

While original thinkers try to come up with unique ideas, elaborate thinkers produce many details.

Elaboration: Embellish, Enhance, Enrich

Young children delight in the detail in the *Where's Waldo?* book series. In these books, Martin Handford uses highly detailed drawings to create elaborate scenes and hide objects. They are very creative because of their elaboration. Elaboration allows for the addition of significant detail to basic ideas, adding depth to ideas and products. Think of the good books you've read with detailed descriptions of places and people. Think of the detail in music by Bach or Mozart or Chopin. Think of the detail in Gothic architecture. These are all examples of elaboration.

Some activities that encourage elaborative thinking include the following:

1. Create sentences filled with alliteration (e.g., Hattie Henderson hated happy healthy hippos; Patsy Planter plucked plump, purple, plastic plums.)

2. Read poems that include even more detail than you want to know, such as Shel Silverstein's, "Sara Cynthia Sylvia Stout Would Not Take the Garbage Out." (A quick search on the Internet will find the poem in print.)

3. Give members of the family blank pieces of paper and pencils, crayons, or markers. Instruct each person to draw a simple house by sketching a square with a triangle on top of it for the roof. Next, set a timer for 5 minutes. During the allotted time, each person should add as many details to the picture as possible. At the end of the 5 minutes, share the pictures and talk about them. Encourage children to add more details as they see/hear ideas that they like. The object is to make the pictures as elaborate as possible.

4. Sit down at the computer. Have your child take a seat next to you. (You are going to do the typing.) Write a simple sentence, such as, "The boy walked down the street." Next, the two of you generate questions and answers that will allow for the elaboration of the story.

Why was the boy walking down the street? Was he by himself or with someone else? Can we replace "walking" with another word? What did the boy see around him? How was he feeling? What was he wearing? Fire the questions out as quickly as possible and insert answers before, in the middle of, and after the original sentence. You and your child will be surprised at how the two of you can turn a simple sentence into an elaborate story.

5. Have your child help plan a party, including invitations, decorations, games, food, and entertainment. Use everyday materials that are found around the house. The more detailed the better. This party can be for people, pets, or stuffed animals. It might be fun to have a theme into which each item must fit.

6. Review classified ads and human interest stories with your young person. Look for ideas that evoke images for a story. Take turns creating stories based on the mental images created from the ads. For example, a classified you create might read, "Lost—Bag of pearls in blue velvet bag somewhere between Main Street and 7th Avenue after large dog grabbed it out of owner's hand. If found, please call 555-5983." What kind of story can be created using elements from this ad? What kind of a person would walk around with a bag of pearls? How did the person acquire the pearls? What was the person going to do with the pearls? The possibilities for a great story are endless.

7. Encourage students to put lots of detail into their school projects, when appropriate.
8. When your young person tells you something, encourage him to explain more with statements like, "Tell me more."

SCAMPER: PUTTING IT ALL TOGETHER

One way to combine all of these elements of creativity together is to use the acronym SCAMPER when thinking about a problem or project. SCAMPER stands for:

Substitution—Can I put something in place of something else?

Combination—Can I combine two ideas into one?

Adapt—How could I make something similar work?

Modify or **M**agnify—How can I alter or expand the use of this idea?

Put to other use—What other applications is this idea useful for?

Eliminate—What parts of the idea can I get rid of?

Rearrange or **R**everse—How can I rearrange the components? What are some opposite ideas?

SCAMPER helps you and your child develop creativity by combining many elements of creative thinking together. This strategy can be useful when trying to come up with original school products and projects as well.

CONCLUSION

Enjoy the creativity in your children. Know that with your support, the traits of fluency, flexibility, originality, and elaboration will help them to become productive individuals and good problem solvers as adults.

6

THERE'S MORE THAN ONE
WAY TO EDUCATE A CHILD

WHAT makes a good academic environment for gifted kids? Does your neighborhood school provide the best for your highly able children? Should you consider different options? What are all the ways you can contribute to your young person's education?

An appropriate academic setting for a very bright child is determined not just by the school, but by the child's total environment. I remember working at one school where a parent was upset with her child's classroom teacher. I understood the parent's frustration, as the teacher could have been doing much more to enrich and advance the student's learning. Because I lacked authority to change the classroom situation, I suggested some things that the parent might do at home to help. The mother's response was, "The education of my child is not my job. That's the school's job. It is my job to love my child and have fun with her—not to educate her." I was shocked by this answer. Although it is the school's job to educate every student, no matter his ability, it also is the parents' responsibility.

A good academic environment at home and at school is one where there is a culture of high expectations with lots of support in place. Because of a combination of funding and philosophy, the academic needs of bright students often are expected to be met in the regular classroom, as opposed to special classes or schools. Because the abilities of gifted students are on a continuum, it may or may not be possible to meet their needs in the regular classroom. (It is doubtful that the academic needs of highly gifted kids could be met this way.) Whether or not the regular classroom will offer enough challenge also depends on the population of the school. If students, in general, perform above grade level it will be much easier than if the population, in general, performs below grade level. All schools are not created equal.

Even with the best situations, certain things must be in place if gifted students are able to be appropriately served in the regular classroom. Support needs to come from everyone: administration, teachers, parents, and students.

Administrators must make decisions that offer the necessary building blocks for good schools. They need to:

- hire highly competent teachers;
- provide teachers with opportunities to further their education in meeting the needs of all populations, including the gifted;
- encourage teachers to attend gifted conferences; and
- expect teacher evaluations to show evidence that academic provisions have been made for highly capable students.

Teachers need to be prepared for the academic diversity within the regular classroom and be confident and creative. They also must:

- have high expectations for themselves, for students, and for parents;
- continuously acquire education in the field of gifted education and in ways to differentiate instruction;
- continuously assess students (formally and informally) and analyze ways to meet the changing needs of students;
- collaborate with colleagues to find the best possible educational strategies; and
- support the positive steps that are taken by administrators, other teachers, parents, and students, keeping an open mind about different educational approaches.

Parents offer continuity and support from the time their children are born through adulthood. This includes setting up the culture of learning and its importance. Parents need to:

- provide a home environment where kids feel safe and loved;
- guide children to have strong character traits and values;
- expose young people to a wide variety of experiences so that they may get a taste of the possibilities of life;
- show excitement both about their own learning and the experiences of their children;
- reflect on the things they read and share those reflections with youngsters;

- read to children, even as they get older;
- encourage respectful family discussions realizing that everyone does not need to agree;
- help youngsters to develop their own lifetime philosophy rather than dictating one;
- show support for their child's school by attending conferences and school meetings, helping in the classroom, helping with fundraising, and serving on committees;
- be respectful of teachers, administrators, and parents when speaking to children; and
- expect that young people will pay attention in school, hand in assignments on time, go beyond what is expected, and be considerate of others.

Students have, perhaps, the most important role of all. Too often, we expect the adults to assume all of the responsibility for the young person's education and well-being. Although it certainly is important to have that support, the desire to learn ultimately needs to come from the child. If it does not, learning will not become a lifelong process. Students need to:
- enjoy learning;
- feel that a good education is important;
- be willing to work hard and go beyond what is asked of them;
- look for learning experiences in all situations—even in those they do not like;
- hand in assignments on time;
- create their own learning experiences when necessary;

- have strong character and values; and
- be respectful and tolerant of others.

VOLUNTEERING AT SCHOOL

Certainly part of a good educational environment includes the cooperation and integration of home and school. One way to accomplish this is to volunteer to help out at your child's school.

Sometimes well-meaning parents tell a teacher that they would like to help in their child's classroom and then feel left out when the teacher never calls. It may be helpful for parents to look at the teacher's perspective on volunteering. Teachers may be hesitant to call on parents because they don't know the competency of or comfort level of the parent. Teachers also may have had experiences in the past where they counted on a parent to be present and then, at the last minute, the parent cancelled. Sometimes, educators are concerned that volunteers will talk about individuals or groups of children with other parents, betraying confidentiality. The teacher also may be concerned that the parent will judge her teaching abilities and techniques unfairly. Often, the teacher may feel like it's more work than it's worth to put something together for the parent to do and then have to train the parent to do certain tasks.

Creating extra work for the teacher is an especially big issue. Let's use the analogy of a sick friend to demonstrate how you can effectively help your child's teacher.

If you have a friend who is sick or in trouble, you may say, "Just let me know if there is anything I can do to help." Usually, you will not be called. However, if you say, "I know you are going through a difficult time right now, so I'm coming over to your house on Saturday to clean for 2 hours," or " I will bring dinner over on Wednesday night," your help is much more likely to actually be accepted.

If you just offer to help in a general way at school, you may get the same nonresponse as you did with your sick friend. Instead, approach the teacher with a specific need and suggestion. For instance, "It must be very difficult for you to work with all of your math students. Recently, I saw a great idea for . . . I would love to help you by working with a small group of students on this. Is there a good time for me to come in each week to assist?" Once you offer to do something, be there every week and on time. Teachers need to be able to depend on you.

Think about any specific skills, interests, or hobbies that you may have. Is there a way you might use your knowledge to work with an individual child, a small group of students, or an entire class? Hopefully, if you take the focus off of your child and help the teacher where he needs it the most, the teacher will have more time to accommodate the needs of your child.

If you do volunteer in the classroom:
- Be respectful of the teacher's time.
- Whenever possible, come to her with suggestions of things you might do to help.
- Always show up at your appointed time. If anything, be a couple of minutes early.

- Do not talk about your experiences with students with other parents.

Does your school offer before and afterschool classes? If not, can you help start a program by working with the principal or the school's parent organization? Doing so can provide enrichment opportunities not only for your student, but many others. Classes may be taught by volunteer parents or you may hire qualified instructors. Sometimes fees are paid by attending students and sometimes they are subsidized through parent organizations or grants. A few of the many possibilities include chess club, math club, Junior Great Books, foreign languages, puzzle club, inventions, knitting, geography club, hobby club, acting, and dance. In Chapter 7 you will find many suggestions for supporting specific subjects, including academic competitions. Any of these ideas for support would be a good basis on which to create before and afterschool clubs or classes.

Parents with rigid work schedules have a greater challenge volunteering at school, but there still are possibilities. Is there something you can do at home to help out, such as make phone calls, put together a class newsletter, or do research on the Internet? Can you help to raise money for programs and materials?

Whatever well-thought-out and committed volunteering that parents provide at or for the school frees up time for teachers to dedicate to students, offers additional opportunities for kids, or adds to the educational coffers. Volunteering is an important way to contribute to a good academic environment.

SCHOOLING OPTIONS

If you come away with nothing else after reading this book, I hope it will be that there is no one right way to educate a child; there are only choices. The need for some nontraditional methods may be dictated by special circumstances. If your student is globally very bright or highly gifted, if your young person is particularly gifted in one subject, or if he has strong interests in a nonacademic area, the conventional learning environment may need to be altered.

Sasha is an example of a student with a special talent in one area. She was a real actress. From the time she was very young, she loved to dress up in costumes and pretend she was someone else. Performing in front of others was such a treat for her. Recognizing this interest, her parents enrolled her in a local drama group, which then led to her having a walk-on part in a play put on by a community theater group. One opportunity followed another and by the time she was in upper elementary school she was paid for acting parts in legitimate theater. This cut into her school day severely. Sometimes the plays kept her up very late at night. Sometimes she had to travel out of town with touring productions. Nontraditional accommodations needed to be made for Sasha. Her parents worked with the school to allow the child to make up work when not able to be present and to have a tutor to help her keep up with her classwork. Sasha had a real talent in acting and she was allowed to develop that while altering the academic environment.

Another example is Eric. At age 16, Eric was very interested in science. In fact, he had been working in a lab at a local pharmaceutical firm on Saturdays for the past 6 months. His parents realized his need to progress much faster in science than was possible in the local school. Eric resisted making any of the changes his parents suggested because he had a couple of very close friends at school and he didn't want to be separated from them. Eventually, they worked out a compromise where the boy remained in his regular classes for most of the time, continued working at the lab on Saturdays, and then also was able to communicate with a mentor scientist in another state over the Internet.

There can be a host of other reasons why traditional education may not meet some or any of your needs. What should parents do? How can both their child's academic and social needs be met? Parents certainly should try to work with local school systems to brainstorm all possible accommodations, but they also need to understand that they have other choices. They never should assume that any choice will be a panacea; instead, they need to understand the advantages and disadvantages of each. Some of the many possible options for schooling gifted children, along with advantages and disadvantages of each option, are described on the next few pages. Please note that many of these options can overlap with one another and many can be combined. As you read through the rest of this book, you will see many examples of ways the options can be blended. The combinations are restricted only by your imagination.

Neighborhood School

In general, when speaking of the neighborhood school, one is referring to the building in the traditional public school system that serves the child's home area.

ADVANTAGES

This is certainly the most convenient possibility. The school is close. It is probably either within walking distance or transportation is provided. The school often has before and afterschool options, which may be helpful for working parents. Children become acquainted with others in the neighborhood, making it easier to make friends. A bright child may feel confident knowing that he is one of the better academic students in the school. He may be exposed to a wide variety of types of people and, hopefully, learn to get along with those who come from different socioeconomic backgrounds, ethnicities, and intellectual abilities.

DISADVANTAGES

A gifted child may not find a cadre of intellectual peers at her local school. She may feel very lonely and set apart from others at the school. Teachers and/or the organization of the school may not be equipped to provide for the higher intellectual needs of the student; therefore, she may not feel intellectually challenged.

Open Enrollment School

Open-enrollment policies allow a student to transfer to the public school of his or her choice. There are two basic types of open-enrollment policies in place in the states—intradistrict and interdistrict. Intradistrict open-enrollment policies allow a student to transfer to another school within his or her school district. Interdistrict open-enrollment policies allow a student to transfer to a school outside his or her home district, but often require both the sending district and the receiving district to agree to participate.

ADVANTAGES

If you are not happy with your neighborhood school, you may have the option of enrolling your child in a school that is out of your neighborhood. Another school may offer a stronger academic program.

DISADVANTAGES

You probably will have to provide transportation for your child. Because the school may be some distance away, it may be more difficult for your young person to connect with friends there.

Special School for the Gifted (Public or Private)

This is a school with a special focus on academics for students of high ability. It most likely is not a neighborhood school. There usually are rigid entrance requirements and often more support is expected from parents.

ADVANTAGES

Because the school is designed for the gifted, the curriculum hopefully will be rigorous and stimulating. Your child will have intellectual peers and academic challenges. He may be better prepared to go on to the next level of education. You should expect teachers to be trained specifically to work with very bright children and cover not only more content, but higher level thinking skills.

DISADVANTAGES

Transportation may be a problem. There may be additional costs, even if the school is public. Your child may not be exposed to as great a diversity of children as at your neighborhood school.

Your child may feel intellectually average or even below average amongst so many smart kids. High expectations may feel too challenging and stressful.

Dual Enrollment

Dual enrollment is where a student is enrolled in two separate, academically related institutions. For instance, the young person may be enrolled in middle school, but take some classes at the high school. Or, the student may still be a high school student, but also take classes at a college or university.

ADVANTAGES

When a student enrolls in two levels at once, his education automatically is accelerated. Dual enrollment is useful for students who have exhausted the academic possibilities in a specific area at their regular school. For instance, once a student has taken all of the higher level math courses available at the high school level, she can move on and take a more advanced math class at a local college or university. Therefore, while taking most of her classes at high school, she takes one math class at college. For some, dual enrollment may ease the transition to high school or to college. In addition, dual enrollment is seen by parents as a money saving strategy, with students earning college credits while still at home. In some states, the law requires the school district to pay for these more advanced classes.

Although a student may be academically ready for advancement, she may not be ready emotionally or socially. College courses are rigorous, and students can get in over their heads. Students normally have to pay for any textbooks, which can be very expensive. If college courses are offered only on the actual college campus, the student will be responsible for travel to and from the campus.

Early Admission

Early admission can occur both at kindergarten and college. At the kindergarten level, a student begins school before the traditional age. (This is not permitted by all schools and even where it is permitted, careful screening is necessary.)

Early admission also can take place for gifted teenagers who have exhausted their high school curriculum. Some of these students have met state graduation requirements by the end of their sophomore or junior year. Early admission programs allow these students to skip their senior year and go on to college.

In rare cases, early entrance programs offer the opportunity to start college or university work at an even younger age—some as early as age 12. These students may never attend traditional high schools. Essentially these are programs that take bright students and radically accelerate them into full-time college studies while maintaining a supportive environment to help make sure they succeed. In order to be successful in these programs, students must be both intelligent and mature.

ADVANTAGES

For students who are both academically and emotionally/socially advanced, entering kindergarten early may enable them to begin school at a time that is most appropriate for them.

The same may be true for students who enter college 1 to 6 years early. In addition, these students will have the option of finishing graduate school before their age peers finish college, giving them a head start on their careers. They will be able to concentrate on academics while many of their age-mates are dealing more with adolescent social issues.

DISADVANTAGES

Caution must be used to make certain that students are both intelligent and mature. Even highly gifted, mature students may decide not to take this route because they want to be with their friends and participate in high school sports and other activities such as band or athletics.

PARENT RESOURCES: EARLY ADMISSION

- Berger, S. L. (2006). *College planning for gifted students: Choosing and getting into the right college.* Waco, TX: Prufrock Press.

  Discusses all aspects of preparing for college, including information on early entrance programs.
- Muratori, M. C. (2006). *Early entrance to college: A guide to success.* Waco, TX: Prufrock Press.

  Factors affecting academic, social, and emotional adjustment to college are explored and information about early entrance programs in the United States is provided.

- Early Entrance College Programs in the U.S.—http://www.earlyentrance.org/Home

  This Web site compares a variety of schools that accept groups of students at least a year before they would typically go to college. A long list of testimonials (both positive and negative) is included.
- Hoagies' Gifted Education Page: Early Entrance College Programs—http://www.hoagiesgifted.org/early_college.htm

  Lists specific schools and also success stories.

Homeschooling

Homeschooling is learning outside of the public or private school environment. Education takes place not only at home, but often through resources available in the community and through interactions with other families who homeschool. It involves a commitment by a parent or guardian to completely oversee his or her student's educational development. Different states have different regulations for this schooling option. If you are considering homeschooling, be sure and check with your state department of education for rules.

ADVANTAGES

When a child is educated at home, he can focus on his real strengths. He may advance much more quickly through curriculum and also go more in depth with it. It often is the best choice for highly gifted young people. There may be more time to pursue the study of a musical instrument or some other nonacademic interest area. There are more opportunities to visit museums and other outside educational venues. The student may be spared from dealing with others who may be unkind or have different values than your family.

DISADVANTAGES

Homeschooling is a very large commitment on the part of the parent or guardian. This choice may not be possible if both parents work outside the home or the child is from a single parent home. Parents may not have the teaching skills to effectively homeschool their child. Parents need to work harder to provide social interaction. The child may not have the opportunity to learn to deal with students who are unkind or have different values than his family.

PARENT RESOURCES: HOMESCHOOLING

- Hoagies' Gifted Education Page: Homeschool Curricula—http://www.hoagiesgifted.org/homeschool_curricula.htm
  List of homeschool curricula with Internet links that have been used successfully by homeschooling gifted.
- Homeschooling With Gifted Children—http://www.hsc.org
  You will find a wealth of information here that is provided by the Homeschool Association of California. It includes reasons for homeschooling your gifted child, how to actually do it, working with teens, preparing for college, working with gifted children who have learning difficulties, and a list of resources.

- Internet Resources for Homeschooling Highly Gifted Students—http://www.hollingworth.org/homesc.html

    This site includes listservs, Web sites, electronic magazines, bibliographies, and research studies—all on homeschooling gifted children.
- Ontario Gifted Homeschooling—http://www.ontariogifted.org/homesch.htm

    At this site you will find a message board, supportive articles, sources for supplies, and suggestions for curriculum.
- Rivero, L. (2002). *Creative home schooling: A resource guide for smart families.* Scottsdale, AZ: Great Potential Press.

Full-Time Tutoring

Picture the old plantation in the South with the children in the family sitting under the large tree with their tutor. It was almost like the one-room schoolhouse, with the tutor dedicated to the education of the youngsters. Some families still do hire full-time teachers for this personalized type of education. Tutors often are hired by families whose employment or frequent travel do not allow children to attend school on a regular basis.

ADVANTAGES

This choice frees the up family for a very flexible schedule and geographic location. It offers an opportunity to tailor the child's education.

It is costly, and it may be difficult to find a qualified tutor. If not handled properly, it may be an isolating experience for the child.

Part-Time Tutoring

Hiring someone to work one-on-one with a child is a fairly common occurrence. Part-time tutors are sometimes hired to work with a child during regular school hours at the student's home school, but more frequently they work with the child outside of the school day.

Advantages

A part-time tutor may be used to enrich a child's education, to answer questions of advanced students about their regular school studies, or to help them study a topic in-depth.

Disadvantages

Obtaining a part-time tutor may be costly. It may be difficult to find a tutor who understands and works well with gifted students.

Distance Learning

Distance learning is a formalized teaching and learning system specifically designed to be carried out remotely by using electronic communication. It most often is accomplished using the Internet, including audio, video, e-mail, and other interactive technologies that are constantly evolving.

Advantages

Distance learning may be used for one course or a student's entire school experience. One often can maintain a very flexible schedule with online classes, working any time of the day or night. Some students create more thoughtful responses to assignments because they have more time to consider their answers. There often are opportunities to form Internet friendships with like minds from all over the world, because there are no geographic boundaries to this type of learning. Online options may be a good choice for students who live in rural areas where small populations may limit the number of high-level classes available, families who travel for extended periods of time, homeschoolers, individuals whose talents in sports or the arts cause them to have unusual schedules, students who need to accelerate their learning beyond what is offered in their home school, and students who need to work to help support the family.

Disadvantages

This form of education is still in its infancy and is, therefore, constantly improving. Some students may find it difficult to discipline themselves to keep up with assignments. Some will have problems because their keyboarding skills are not adequate. It may be an isolating experience, and it may be costly.

PARENT RESOURCES: DISTANCE LEARNING

- Center for Talent Development at Northwestern University—http://www.ctd.northwestern.edu/learning/description.html

    Programs are offered for academically talented students in enrichment, high school honors, and Advanced Placement (AP) courses.

- Center for Talented Youth at Johns Hopkins University—http://cty.jhu.edu

    CTY focuses on the needs of students with high and exceptionally high academic abilities.

- The Education Program for Gifted Youth (EPGY) at Stanford University—http://epgy.stanford.edu

    EPGY provides high-ability students of all ages with individualized educational experiences, optimized in both pace and content.

- eLearners.com—http://www.elearners.com/resources/k12-online.asp

    At this site you will find links to state-level virtual schools. It should be noted that not all of these schools will offer classes suitable for gifted students.

- National Charter School Clearinghouse—http://www.ncsc.info

    Use this database by typing in the words Virtual Charter Schools in the search box. Again, these may or may not be appropriate for gifted learners.

- Stanford University EPGY Online High School—http://epgy.stanford.edu/ohs

    This is an online, 3-year, diploma granting, independent high school for gifted students.

- Virtual High School—http://www.govhs.org

  If you check out the catalog, you will see that there are high school courses available to middle schoolers. These classes are designed for gifted and talented students who meet all course prerequisites.

With knowledge about the many choices for possible options for school, parents can make the best choices for educational environments for their family.

SPECIALTY PROGRAMS

If, when selecting the appropriate educational environment for your family, you choose to stay with the neighborhood school or a specialty school, it is helpful to know that some of these will have specialty programs available for high-ability learners. Entrance requirements to specialty programs may vary from school to school. If your student is not recommended for a program and is motivated, there is nothing wrong with requesting admittance. Just know that, if accepted, you cannot ask that expectations be lowered. Some of the many specialty programs include those detailed in the following sections.

Honors Classes

The definition of honors classes can vary from school to school, so make certain you ask questions and understand its local meaning. Generally speaking, an honors class parallels the curriculum offered in the corresponding regular class, but may cover additional topics or some topics in greater depth.

Advanced Placement (AP) Classes

Advanced Placement (AP) classes (http://www.collegeboard.com/student/testing/ap/about.html), administered by The College Board and taught at many high schools, allow students to participate in college-level courses. As of this writing, there are 37 courses and exams available across 22 subject areas. By achieving certain scores on exams, students may get college credit. If your local high school offers AP courses, only a handful may be offered. Many people do not realize that students can take AP exams even if they are not enrolled in formal classes. Instead, they can obtain the necessary materials and study on their own. AP classes also can be taken online.

International Baccalaureate (IB) Programme

The International Baccalaureate (IB) Programme (http://www.ibo.org) long has been recognized as a rigorous high school curriculum for students who are academically talented. Many gifted students search out high schools that offer this program because they know it prepares them well for admittance to selective colleges.

What many people do not realize is that there are also programs available for elementary and middle school students. The Primary Years Programme (ages 3–12) and the Middle Years

Programme (ages 11–16) are becoming more and more prevalent. Each of these levels provides a truly international curriculum.

To become an IB school, teachers and administrators go through special training and schools only can offer the IB curriculum if they are approved by the organization. Once accepted, schools are reevaluated on a set schedule. Curriculum is taught through a transdisciplinary approach. An emphasis is placed on students:

- learning to ask challenging questions,
- learning how to learn,
- developing a strong sense of their own identity and culture, and
- developing the ability to communicate with and understand people from other countries and cultures.

When looking for the best educational environment for your child, be sure to investigate these specialty programs at your school or consider having your student open enroll at a school that does have them.

MENTORS

Yet another option for creating an optimal educational environment is the use of a mentor. Mentors are individuals who work one-on-one with a student on either a special interest or a specific area of academics. Mentors are able to offer very specific support and guidance that would not be possible from a regular teacher or parent. There are many stories of very successful relationships between mentors and their protégés. It often is a very special relationship.

Eric is one example of a student who benefited from having a mentor. Eric was a 15-year-old who lived in a small town in a Western state. He loved both the peacefulness and the physical activities associated with the nearby mountains. Although his parents enjoyed the serenity of their little paradise, they did not share Eric's enthusiasm for the rugged backcountry experiences that were available.

Down the road lived a well-known outdoor photographer who had a lot of heavy equipment (tripods, cameras, lenses, and camping gear) that needed to be schlepped into the hills to take pictures. He needed a good hand. Eric fit the bill. The two paired up and Eric became the photographer's Sherpa. Although the cameraman got Eric to help him carry his equipment, the arrangement also was very beneficial to the teenager. The boy not only filled his need for backcountry hiking, but he also learned about the flora and fauna of the area, outdoor survival skills, and a great deal about photography from this man. In addition, Eric gained a lot of self-confidence and deepened his love of nature. The photographer had become the boy's mentor.

Mentors can come from many sources. For instance, Jenna was a 10-year-old math whiz. In general, she was good student, but at math, she really excelled. Because she was definitely above grade level with her skills and understanding of the subject, she attended math class with the sixth graders rather than her fifth-grade classmates. In spite of this accommodation, Jenna still did not feel challenged. After a brainstorming session among her teachers, it was decided to explore some other options. Their ideas included the following possibilities of people with whom Jenna could work on more advanced, enriching math activities:

- Advanced math student at a nearby high school—High schools often require students to volunteer for community service. One of Jenna's teachers would talk to the head of the math department at the high school to see if any advanced students were available and willing to work with Jenna.

- University student—A local university offered majors both in math and in education. One of Jenna's teachers would check with the heads of both departments to see if that would be a possibility.

- Parent—Teachers wondered if there were any parents at the school who loved math and would be willing to work with Jenna. At the next staff meeting, the other teachers at the school would be surveyed to see if they know of any school parents who have strong backgrounds in math plus a willingness to work with a student.

- Community member—Some companies encourage employees to participate in community service. Jenna's teachers asked if any local companies had employees who were strong in math. One of the teachers was designated to contact the HR departments of a number of companies to ask.

Businesses, law firms, and hospitals all use mentoring systems to help young recruits as they start out in their professions. It makes good sense to also use this technique with kids who have strong abilities and could use some guidance and tutelage.

There are many reasons to establish mentoring relationships and many possible ways to structure them. Students who might benefit from such a relationship include:

- those having progressed beyond the curriculum offered at school and who need more in-depth study;
- young people wanting to pursue a specific area of focus;
- those needing help determining a career choice; and
- smart children who have special needs because they are English Language Learners, have physical problems, or experience socioeconomic differences.

A mentoring relationship will not meet the needs of every gifted student. Before going through the work of setting up a mentorship, one must ask seriously if there is a valid reason for doing so and if there is enough of a commitment on the part of both the mentor and the protégé to make it successful.

In *Developing Mentorship Programs for Gifted Students* (Siegle, 2005), practical strategies for starting and developing a mentoring program are presented. These include structuring a program, selecting a mentor, monitoring progress, and ensuring success.

Although mentorship sometimes is arranged through schools, more often mentorships are arranged by a parent. The relationship can work at all age levels. Below are some examples of how mentorships have been successfully arranged in a variety of situations.

Elementary School

In one elementary school, parents and teachers decided that some of their students would benefit from the enriching experience of a mentorship program. In the end, it was very successful, but only lasted as long as a couple of dedicated parents put in long hours and creative efforts to make it work. With their busy schedules, the teachers did not have the time to set up this program. However, the parents were motivated and anxious to help. The following steps were taken to set up the program:

- Teachers and parents were surveyed to find students who had significant interests in subjects that went beyond the scope of the curriculum. This was evidenced by passion in a specific subject for a minimum of 2 years.

- Each student who had a strong, long-term interest was asked if he would like to participate in a mentoring program.

- A parent volunteer searched for someone who might address the needs of that particular student. The circle of possibilities started close, asking teachers and parents if they knew of anyone who might be appropriate and then branching out from there to businesses, museums, universities, and other community groups.

- Once a potential mentor was found, the mentor, student, and parent met to make certain that they felt comfortable with one another.

- An agreement was signed to meet outside of the school building and outside of school hours for 10 times. (Many of the mentoring relationships went on long beyond that, but it is important to have an initial time limit so that no one feels trapped by a long commitment.)

- Legal issues between the school and mentor were discussed. (These issues vary from district to district and often revolve around safety and liability.)
- Parents addressed any concerns they had about leaving their child with someone they didn't know well.

Examples of successful mentorships that took place using this arrangement included:

- Sam, who was interested in snakes, was paired with a herpetologist from the zoo.
- Francine, who had an affinity for cartooning, was paired with a political cartoonist from a local newspaper.
- Gilda, who was gifted in music and had been taking classical piano lessons for years, was paired with a jazz musician.
- Zain, who was very good at computers, was paired with an IT person who helped him build a computer using discarded parts. The two also explored programming.

After the individual mentorships were concluded, mentors, parents, and students were surveyed to determine the level of satisfaction. Appropriate signs of appreciation were bestowed upon the participants. Many of the mentors who participated in this program were initially skeptical about how it would work. Almost without exception, when the mentorships were finished, the adults said that they felt they got at least as much satisfaction from it as the young people. Although at first the mentors were concerned about how they would plan for the get-togethers, they soon found that, because the children had been so well-screened, the natural curiosities of the youngsters drove the meetings with little effort.

Middle School

A successful middle school mentor program (Fertig, 2006; Machuk, 2006) was originally started by two mothers who felt their children would benefit from the added mental stimulation.

Students were selected by their teachers. Individual young people were paired with an architect, a doctor, several writers, a biathlon coach, a municipal counselor, a veterinarian, a couple of artists, a theatrical makeup expert, a lawyer, a carpenter, two photographers, an interior designer, several computer experts, and a cartoonist. These community members met with each child for 2 hours each week over an 8–10 week period. At the end of the program, students prepared presentations for their classmates. These young people accomplished a variety of tasks under the tutelage of their mentors, including building a ski rack, mastering an architectural drafting program, and working at a veterinary hospital.

Those in charge of the program said that they were surprised that it wasn't that difficult to find community members to volunteer their time to help the students and that the program was very fulfilling to the mentors, as well as the young people.

High School—Science

When you read about winners of very selective competitions, such as the Intel Science Talent Search or the Siemens Competition in Math, Science, and Technology, you will find that most of the participants had mentors to guide them in their research.

Mentors at this level require much more expertise as students already have a large storehouse of knowledge. Students may benefit from work in specific topics within a subject, especially if they have a deep interest and have already exceeded the school's offerings. Mentors may guide students in the research of narrowed fields and also may help the student sort out career possibilities.

Finding good mentors at this level may require some real digging. You can start locally, but in this age of technology, mentoring also can take place electronically, so you may want to broaden your horizons. Some possible places to start are institutions, universities, professional organizations, specialty clubs, journals, and competition judges.

The scientific research society, Sigma Xi, has a Web-based pilot program (http://www.sigmaxi.org/programs/education/men.high.shtml) to locate and support mentors for three specialty math and science high schools in North Carolina, South Carolina, and Illinois. The program offers advice, training, and general information to mentors or potential mentors and an extensive list of other resources and programs related to mentoring at all educational levels. Even if your student does not attend one of the schools that this group supports, you will find extensive, helpful information at their site.

Amber Hess (n.d.) is a passionate science student who has won awards at many prestigious science competitions. She was an Intel Science Talent Search Finalist, a semifinalist for the Siemens Westinghouse competition, and she won a First Place Grand Award in Chemistry at the Intel International Science and Engineering Fair (ISEF). She qualified to compete at the California State Science Fair five times, winning fourth, third, and two first-place awards. Hess went on to attend MIT where she majored in chemical engineering. She stresses the importance of a mentor/advisor, stating that the vast majority of winners of top fairs have mentors and the vast majority of students have to find their own mentors.

Hess (n.d.) gives specific steps for finding a mentor and stresses the importance of students finding their own mentors. It is, she states, the only way they'll appreciate the advisor. She also feels strongly that mentors respond when contacted by motivated students, not motivated teachers. Among her suggestions are the following:

- Determine your general areas of interest.
- Search the Web sites of research universities for scientists in departments of your area of interest. You want someone who is actively publishing research in their field.
- At the department Web site for the university, bring up and read the faculty bios.
- Once you've gathered 20–30 professors' bios, research them one by one. Find recent articles written by the

professor. You want to understand if this person is doing the right type of research for you and you also want to be knowledgeable when contacting the individual.

- Draft a personalized e-mail in which you identify yourself, your school, and what specifically about the scientist's research interests you. Do not say that you want that person to be your mentor, but request a meeting where you can learn more about the scientist's research.

- Have someone proofread and edit the letter. Send it out and hope for the best. You may go through many rejections before you find someone who wants to help you.

- If you receive a positive response, set up a meeting date. At that meeting you should bring everything that you've found on the scientist's research and a couple of thoughtful questions about it. If the rapport seems good and you find this person's area of expertise interesting, ask "Do you need any help in your lab?"

High School—Other Academic Areas

Finding a mentor while still in high school in an area other than science may require a more creative approach. Remember that at this level, a student would not even seek out a mentor unless he had a highly specialized interest and/or all courses available had already been exhausted. But, mentors may be found by first:

- joining an organization (e.g., photography club, geology club, writer's group);
- taking a specialty class (e.g., acting, art, computer);
- taking private lessons (e.g., instrumental);
- getting a job in an area of interest (e.g., caddy at a golf club; work at a hospital, a museum, or a theatre);
- volunteering;
- spreading the word through your house of worship; and
- finding Internet groups that support the specialty area.

By putting oneself in an environment where there are people with similar interests, a student may find someone who will take him under his wing. Sometimes teachers who are paid (such as music teachers) become valuable mentors. Even though a teacher is paid to teach specific skills, that same teacher also may turn into a wonderful friend and guide. Also, students and teachers should let others know of a special interest and a desire to find a mentor in a specific field. Whoever you tell may know someone who knows someone.

Special Circumstances

No matter what the age, bright students with special needs due to physical problems, socioeconomic differences, or trying to assimilate into the American culture while learning English also may benefit from a mentor to help see the possibilities beyond the present environment.

A young person with any of these circumstances can benefit from working with a person who has had similar special needs and has gone on to be very successful.

In *Multicultural Mentoring of the Gifted and Talented* (Torrance, Goff, & Satterfield, 1997), the creation of a mentorship program for ethnically diverse, economically disadvantaged youth is presented. The book covers a step-by-step process, including a discussion of racial and cultural differences and typical strengths of disadvantaged youth, ideas for creating a mentoring program, identification of mentors and protégés, developing relationships, putting ideas into practice and products, and strategies for evaluating the program.

Students who are underachievers for unknown reasons also may benefit from having mentors. These students most likely will be helped by good relationships with adults who also may help with any deficits the students have acquired and recognize their strengths.

COMBINING SCHOOL OPTIONS

Various school options discussed in this chapter also can be combined with one another. For example, many homeschooling parents combine lessons at home with enrollment in a nearby community college or distance learning courses. Some have their students attend electives such as art or drama at their neighborhood schools. Several examples of combining school options follow.

In second grade, Zach's ability in math was several years above the rest of his class, but his reading was on grade level, and he really needed help with writing. Before Zach was born, his mother had been a middle school math teacher. After consulting with the teachers at the neighborhood school, it was decided that Zach would attend regular classes until 2 p.m. each day. At that time, his mother would take him home and teach him math.

Patricia and Tom Gabrielson had an opportunity to take a year off from work to sail around the world. They knew that this was a unique opportunity that would expose their two children to far more than they could ever get sitting in a classroom. Nevertheless, they wanted to make certain that their kids kept up with the subjects they would miss while away from traditional school. It took a long while, but they were able to find a tutor to travel with them and tailor a curriculum around the experiences the family would have while traveling. They found that Internet access was available in most ports, so they combined the tutoring experience with some online classes.

Even though Aisha was enrolled in a magnet high school for the gifted, the teachers could not meet all of her needs in languages. She had already taken every class available in French and wanted to go on to be much more proficient. So, when she was finished with her classes during the regular school day, she drove over to the local university and took French classes there. Both the high school and the college gave her credit for these additional classes. She also joined the local chapter of Alliance

Française where she met with French speakers each month for dinner or to visit a gallery.

CONCLUSION

Finding the best educational environment for each child in the family may require several different plans. When you do make a decision, be careful not to shut doors behind you. You may try a strategy and find that it doesn't work as well as you hoped. Leave your options open so you can change or reverse your decision if necessary.

It is important to establish a strong, academic environment for your student. If your child is enrolled in a brick and mortar school, support that school in every way possible. At the same time, you need to remember that there are other possibilities available.

7

SPECIFIC SUBJECTS

E ACH young person is unique. Your child may show great strengths across the board or he may do well in only one or several areas. Where he has strengths, support him. Where she is of average ability or shows weaknesses, encourage her. Let's take a look at some specific areas where your child may be particularly able and see what you might do to promote those abilities.

LANGUAGE ARTS

Language arts encompasses the subjects that develop student skills in written and oral language. Gifted children often, but not always, develop an early facilitation for language, including talking early and teaching themselves to read before they enter school.

Parents can encourage expertise in language early on by exposing young people to a broad range of experiences, reading to them on a regular basis, and providing reasons to write. There are many ways that parents can continue to support language arts development as children grow older.

Vocabulary Enrichment and Word Usage

Vocabulary enrichment and word usage at home should be fun and challenging for everyone.

Use big words at the dinner table. Don't talk down to young people. It is only by hearing high-level vocabulary that these words become familiar. Children will figure out the meanings of many words through context. They can ask you about the meanings of the ones they don't understand.

Play family word games together like Scrabble®, Boggle®, and UpWords®. Crossword puzzles and other word puzzles are also fun. These activities increase vocabulary and help kids to look at words in unusual ways. Inexpensive word puzzle books are available in the magazine sections of grocery stores and drug stores. Interactive handheld word games, computer word games, and Internet word games work well for the tech-savvy generation.

Unfortunately, in many K–12 schools, grammar is not taught as it was a generation or two ago. In fact, many younger teachers are very uncomfortable broaching the subject, as it was not something that they were adequately taught when they were students. There are many basic grammar sites at universities that contain the information that was once considered standard fare in middle school. Because of the absence of this subject in schools, all students, including gifted students, often miss out on a key component of their education.

Those who don't have a good grasp of grammar frequently use words incorrectly. We should not deprive intellectually able children of the opportunity to master the English language. Grammar is an essential tool for speaking and writing. (It also is very helpful when trying to attain high scores on college entrance exams.)

If grammar is not embedded in the curriculum at your child's school, make sure you understand the rules and teach them at home. When you hear your student use grammar incorrectly, correct him on the spot and explain whatever rule he broke. If he hears the correction often enough, it will eventually sink into his mind.

Michael Clay Thompson (http://homepage.mac.com/mith/Menu8.html) is a great proponent of presenting strong language arts content to every child, with an emphasis on great literature, Latin-based vocabulary development, and the higher level thinking experiences of traditional grammar. His materials are particularly suited for gifted students. At his Web site you will find files you can download that provide excellent information on grammar and vocabulary.

PARENT RESOURCES: VOCABULARY ENRICHMENT AND WORD USAGE

Interactive Internet Word Games—There are many interactive word game Web sites available. Here are just a few. Each one offers fun games of all abilities that help to build vocabulary and help students see patterns in words.

- Interactive Word Plays—http://www.wordplays.com/p/index

- Dictionary.com—http://dictionary.reference.com/fun
- FunBrain.com—http://www.funbrain.com/words.html
- Vocabulary University—http://www.vocabulary.com
- Merriam-Webster Online—http://www.m-w.com/game/index.htm

Grammar—Grammar provides the foundation for good writing and speaking skills. Each of these sites offers information in a different way.

- OWL (Online Writing Lab)—http://owl.english.purdue.edu/handouts/grammar

  At this site, there is information on grammar, punctuation, and spelling, including computer-driven exercises.

- The Blue Book of Grammar and Punctuation—http://www.grammarbook.com

  Included here are quizzes and an online reference book. There even is a grammar blog.

- Guide to Grammar and Writing—http://grammar.ccc.commnet.edu/grammar

  This link includes all kinds of information on grammar, including words that are often confused, such as affect vs. effect, its vs. it's, and lie vs. lay.

Reading

Gifted children whose strength is reading often teach themselves this skill at remarkably early ages. Parents may be puzzled by this. Without any instruction, some kids just learn to read independently.

One problem that parents of young, precocious readers have is finding and directing their children to books that accommodate their abilities, yet are still age appropriate. Jacob entered kindergarten literally able to read at the highest levels. His parents, not knowing what to do, allowed him to read anything he picked up. He had already read *Dracula* and *Frankenstein* by the time he entered school. What they didn't fully understand was that he was really just 5 years old emotionally and had difficulty distinguishing between reality and fantasy. The books they had allowed him to read had terrified him.

Finding psychologically and developmentally appropriate materials for young, advanced readers can be difficult. Although a 7-year-old child may be reading at a 12- or 14- year-old level, materials that deal with puberty, sex, violence, and other topics are not okay. The best way of knowing what your child is reading is to read it yourself. However, a gifted child can devour books at an enormous rate, making this task nearly impossible. *Some of My Best Friends Are Books: Guiding Gifted Readers From Pre-School to High School* (Halsted, 2002) is a classic resource for finding age-appropriate reading materials. Lists of award-winning books (see Parent Resource box for a listing of various awards given to children's books) can be helpful for finding new material for gifted readers, especially older material that may not be as heavily featured in bookstores as newer titles.

Whether your child is reading years before he starts school or not, there is much you can do to be supportive. Help broaden your youngster's exposure to reading materials by choosing books with enriched vocabulary, topics that cause her to ponder issues, ethnic diversity of subjects and authors, and creative approaches to topics. A children's librarian can become one of your greatest resources—especially if this expert gets to know your child's interests, likes, and dislikes.

Although books are important, there also are many other sources of reading that should be encouraged. There are numerous children's magazines, and as youngsters grow, they should be introduced to newspapers, and appropriate Web sites. For an overview of children's magazines, consult Hoagies' Gifted Education Page: Magazines for Kids (http://www.hoagiesgifted.org/magazines.htm).

Begin reading out loud to children at an early age, and don't stop as the kids develop their own skills. Shared reading is beneficial into the teenage years and beyond. Reading aloud actually used to be considered a standard form of entertainment for adults before radio and television. In addition to reading aloud, talk about the interesting parts of books that each member of the family reads independently. Encourage reading of any kind—magazines, journals, newspapers, and even blogs and Web sites increase a child's knowledge and reading comprehension—sometimes without the child even realizing his or her reading skills are improving. If you value, encourage, and support reading, your excitement about reading will be contagious.

PARENT RESOURCES: READING BOOKLISTS

- Halsted, J. W. (2002). *Some of my best friends are books: Guiding gifted readers from pre-school to high school* (2nd ed.). Scottsdale, AZ: Great Potential Press.

- The Association for Library Service to Children (ALSC)—http://www.ala.org/ala/alsc/awardsscholarships/literaryawds/literaryrelated.cfm

  The ALSC is a division of the American Library Association. It honors excellent books each year in a variety of categories. These awards include:
  o The Newbery Medal—most distinguished contribution to American literature for children;
  o The Caldecott Medal—artist of the most distinguished American picture book for children;
  o Laura Ingalls Wilder Medal—an author or illustrator whose books, published in the United States, have made, over a period of years, a substantial and lasting contribution to literature for children;
  o Mildred L. Batchelder Award—an American publisher for a children's book that was originally published in a foreign language in a foreign country and subsequently translated into English and published in the United States;
  o Pura Belpré Award—a Latino/Latina writer and illustrator whose works best portray, affirm, and celebrate the Latino cultural experience in an outstanding work of literature for children; and
  o Robert F. Sibert Informational Book Medal—the author of the most distinguished informational book published during the preceding year.

- Young Adult Library Services Association (YALSA)—http://www.ala.org/ala/yalsa/booklistsawards/booklistsbook.cfm

  YALSA is a division of the American Library Association that includes awards and book lists for teenagers. The awards and lists include:

- o Alex Awards—adult books that appeal to teen readers;
- o Best Books for Young Adults—annual recommendations for this age group;
- o Margaret A. Edwards Award—recognizes an author's work in helping adolescents become aware of themselves and addresses questions about their role and importance in relationships, society, and in the world;
- o Michael L. Printz Award—an award for a book that exemplifies literary excellence in young adult literature; and
- o Outstanding Books for the College Bound Learner—books on this list offer opportunities to discover new ideas and provide an introduction to a fascinating variety of subjects.

- Gifted Kids, Gifted Characters, and Great Books—http://www.bertiekingore.com/gtchildreninlit.htm

    These books, compiled by Bertie Kingore, are written by authors of merit. Each book contains well-developed characters who display gifted behaviors. The stories include thought-provoking problem situations, issues, or personal needs with which gifted students can identify.

Older readers who don't need a lot of adult supervision may want some system for keeping track of the books they read and ways to communicate with others about their writing. Goodreads (http://www.goodreads.com) offers a great way to do this—and it's free.

I personally use Goodreads to list all of the books I've read and to rate each one. I also can write myself notes about each book. In addition, I can list the titles of books I'm presently reading and have the ability to keep track of what I want to read. I choose to share my information with only a few other friends who are also avid readers and keep track of their books on Goodreads. Your child could choose to keep all information private, share with a few friends, or make her information available to anyone who is a member of Goodreads.

At Goodreads, members have the opportunity to hone their writing skills by writing book reviews, which can then be critiqued by others. There also are discussion threads that allow your student to discuss a particular title.

As a parent, you would want to monitor the way in which your young person uses the site. Although Goodreads is a useful tool, like any public site, it is most appropriate for emotionally mature students who will use it appropriately. If you have elementary or middle school children, you may want to first test the Web site with your own books to see if you are comfortable with it.

These are the parts of Goodreads that I find most beneficial:

- I can list all of the books I have read and rate each on a scale of one to five.
- I can list the dates on which I finished each book.
- I can easily access a summary of a book or information on the author. This is helpful, because sometimes I can't immediately recall the theme of a book I read several years ago.
- By clicking on *edit*, I can record anything I want about the book. Sometimes, I find it helpful to write down

meaningful quotations or passages. Sometimes, I just want to remember a particular impression I had, or cite what I learned from the book. I also can write my own review of the book.

- By clicking on the title of a book I've read, I can see comments that others have made after reading it themselves and click again to see threads of discussion about the book. I also can rate the reviews of others.
- I am able to list books I am in the process of reading and books I want to read.

For those who like to organize information, this is a great way to do it. The books I read become my friends, and when I go back years later and review some of the things I have written about books, the words bring back warm memories.

Goodreads also can be used to form a reading group supervised by a parent or teacher to discuss books read in class or through a homeschool group. This Web site is just one way to be able to organize and voice opinions outside of class.

Writing

The more your child writes, the better she will become at writing. Encourage kids to write diaries, letters, e-mails, stories, and accounts of family vacations. Remember that there are many different types of writing—both fiction and nonfiction—and all are valuable. If your student needs more writing opportunities than offered in his present school setting, consider enrolling him in an online writing class available through The Education Program for Gifted Youth (EPGY) at Stanford University (http://epgy.stanford.edu). Classes are available for students who are ages 9–18. Or, you can check out opportunities through talent search centers at the following sites:

- Duke University's Talent Identification Program—http://www.tip.duke.edu
- Johns Hopkins University's Center for Talented Youth—http://cty.jhu.edu
- Northwestern University's Center for Talent Development—http://www.ctd.northwestern.edu
- University of Denver's Rocky Mountain Talent Search—http://www.du.edu/city

Joining an adult writing group also may offer support and instruction for the writing of an advanced, mature student. A writing group is a gathering of people with a shared interest. The group meets on a regular basis, and often members read and critique one another's work. The format may be quite different for each group, so ask lots of questions about the purpose of the organization and how it is run. To find writing groups in your area, ask a librarian if there are lists of groups available. You can also do an Internet search using the words "writing groups" plus the name of your city and state.

Exploring an online writing forum may be helpful for some older students. Forums are cyberspace discussion groups. Sometimes these forums provide feedback on writing works in progress, and offer a place discuss ideas, share tips and tricks, network, and make friends who have a common interest in writing. As with any online group, parents need to feel comfortable with their young person's participation. Many forums exist and some of them become quite specialized. Do an Internet search on the words "writing forums" and you will be amazed about the choices that come up on your computer screen.

Both summer camps and summer day programs in writing are available. Again, you may want to do an Internet search on "writing camps." Also check out the section on summer experiences in Chapter 4 of this book for other resources.

One more resource is to have your talented and mature student attend a writer's conference. Again, do an Internet search with the words "writer's conference" plus your city and state. Writer's conferences often include informative class-like sessions and also talks given by published writers.

Do you have a young person who is a good writer and also would like to see his writing in print? When students see their writing in print, they often are encouraged, plus it strengthens self-confidence and rewards their personal interest in the subject. Here are some resources that publish student writing; however, if you have a teenage student who is particularly talented, he may want to approach the markets where adults publish. For the mature, older writer, check out the latest edition of *Writers' Market* (http://www.writersmarket.com). You usually can find a recent hard copy of the *Writers' Market* book at your local library. Other sources for publishing student writing are included in the resources box for this section.

PARENT RESOURCES: WRITING

- Dunn, J., & Dunn, D. (2006). *A teen's guide to getting published: Publishing for profit, recognition, and academic success.* Waco, TX: Prufrock Press.

    Two successful former teen authors offer practical writing tips and a list of print and online markets that publish student work.

- Peterson, N. (2006). *Encouraging your child's writing talent: The involved parents' guide.* Waco, TX: Prufrock Press.

    Peterson provides tips to help parents support writing talent, especially in young children.

PLACES THAT PUBLISH STUDENT WRITING

- *Creative Kids*—http://www.prufrock.com/client/client_pages/prufrock_jm_createkids.cfm

    This is the nation's largest magazine by and for kids, publishing creative writing and artwork by kids ages 8–16.

- *New Moon*—http://www.newmoon.org

    This multicultural magazine is written for girls, by girls.

- Scriptito's Place—http://members.aol.com/vangarnews/scriptito.html

    This site is created by Vangar, a publisher of books by children.

- *Stone Soup*—http://www.stonesoup.com

    This is a magazine by young writers and artists.

- "Encourage Student Writing—Publish on the Web!"—http://www.educationworld.com/a_tech/tech/tech042.shtml

    Here you will find numerous opportunities for student publishing on the Internet.

Other writing possibilities in specialized areas are listed under specific subjects in this chapter (e.g., science and history).

Oral Skills: Speech and Debate

No matter how well a presentation or speech is written, the delivery is what the audience remembers. Learning about and practicing volume, stress, pacing, and pronunciation helps students to deliver an oral presentation effectively. An excellent place to turn for model speeches and speech writing is the Web site, American Rhetoric (http://americanrhetoric.com). This is a database of and index to more than 5,000 full text, audio and video versions of public speeches, sermons, legal proceedings, lectures, debates, interviews, other recorded media events, and a declaration or two. It also has identified the 100 most significant American political speeches of the 20th century. Watching and listening to these speeches while observing key points, body language, pauses, intonations, and speed of delivery is very educational.

If your student also is interested in the skills of debate, there are organizations and competitions you may want to pursue. We don't hear a lot about speech and debate competitions for middle and high school students beyond the local level, but where they exist, they provide young people with real-world issues to research and open-ended questions to answer. Speech and debate can greatly improve critical thinking, communication skills, and self-confidence in the public arena.

There are several speech and/or debate organizations you might want to look at. Even if your child's school does not sponsor these opportunities, the Web sites in the Parent Resources box have great methods that can be implemented in family discussions.

PARENT RESOURCES: SPEECH AND DEBATE

- National Forensic League Debate and Speech Honor Society—http://www.nflonline.org/Main/HomePage

     This is the nation's oldest and largest debate and speech honor society.
- National Association for Urban Debate Leagues—http://www.urbandebate.org

     This organization currently works with 311 urban high schools and 51 urban middle schools in school systems with approximately 87% people of color and 78% low-income student populations. Urban Debate Leagues have proven to increase literacy scores by 25%, to improve grade point averages by 8 to 10%, to achieve high school graduation rates of nearly 100%, and to produce college matriculation rates of 71–91%.
- International Debate Education Association (IDEA)—http://www.idebate.org

     IDEA develops, organizes, and promotes debate and debate-related activities in communities throughout the world.

Parents should encourage expertise in all aspects of language arts: vocabulary and word usage, reading, writing, and speech and debate.

MATH

Students who are mathematically gifted are able to go far beyond the math curriculum that is normally offered in schools. For example, Michael was a very smart sixth grader. The previous summer he attended a summer program for kids interested in mathematics at the local university and loved doing the advanced work that he was exposed to there. The regular school he attended didn't have a gifted program. He made good grades in his math class, but he found it too easy. His parents weren't sure how to handle this. They hated to see him bored with something he loved so much last summer.

Ah, a common dilemma!

Michael's parents decided they needed a greater awareness of his abilities. First, they made an appointment to visit with the math teacher at his school. His mom and dad wanted to better understand how the teacher saw Michael as compared to other students in the classroom. They knew that they did not have the same perspective as someone who sees the abilities of many students.

They also wanted to learn more from the district's gifted and talented resource person. (Even if a school doesn't have a gifted program, there still may be a resource person who can help.)

Standardized math tests that had been given by the school district helped to shed some light on Michael's abilities. Typically, students who receive scores at 95% or above should be looked at more carefully; however, even this high of a score only tells us that the student did well on that particular test. It is more important that the student receive high scores on a number of tests, as each assessment covers different types of skills. Students who receive very high scores on tests that are administered at grade level will benefit if they are given an assessment above grade level (i.e., if the student did exceptionally well on the sixth-grade math achievement test given by the district, more may be learned if he were to take the same test at the seventh- or eighth-grade level). It is at this point that one will see a true spread in scores. Some of those students who received the 95% at grade level will show that they did very well for their age group. (A fact we already know.) Others may demonstrate that they are capable of work a year or even several years above their age peers.

Once Michael's parents understood more about his test scores and also had opportunities to meet with his classroom teacher and the gifted and talented resource person, they had a better picture of their son's mathematical abilities. The parents then educated themselves about current research on addressing the needs of high-ability, gifted, and highly motivated students in general and more specifically in math. They wanted to know the true abilities of their son, what the experts recommended, how they could realistically advocate for him at school, and what they could do on their own to contribute to his education.

Although many school districts do not have the money or the personnel to test students above grade level, there are other ways to have off-level testing done. There currently are four programs at universities that conduct regional talent searches incorporating off-level testing. They are:

- Duke University's Talent Identification Program—http://www.tip.duke.edu

- Johns Hopkins University's Center for Talented Youth—http://cty.jhu.edu
- Northwestern University's Center for Talent Development—http://www.ctd.northwestern.edu
- University of Denver's Rocky Mountain Talent Search—http://www.du.edu/city

Each of these universities also offers math opportunities for students who score exceptionally well on these tests. Opportunities may include weekend and summer classes, contests, and e-learning.

Once parents have a good understanding of the math abilities of their child, they can work in tandem with teachers to decide the best option(s) to be used. They may consider acceleration, before and afterschool activities, supplementary materials to be used either at school or home, distance learning, or math competitions. Let's look at each of these.

Acceleration

There are two especially good resources for learning more about acceleration. First, *A Nation Deceived: How Schools Hold Back America's Brightest Students* (http://www.nationdeceived.org), was underwritten by John Templeton Foundation and can be downloaded on the Internet. The report advances the merits of acceleration through 18 forms of acceleration including grade-skipping, early entrance to school, and Advanced Placement (AP) courses. Second, the Institute for Research and

Policy on Acceleration (IRPA; http://www.education.uiowa.edu/belinblank/acceleration) was created to conduct and synthesize research on the cognitive and affective characteristics of academic acceleration. At the Web site you will find questions and answers about acceleration, resources, and stories of acceleration from parents and students.

One word of caution: In the U.S. we often are criticized for having a math curriculum that is "a mile wide and an inch deep." We cover many topics, but we don't study them in depth. Parents without a strong understanding of math often feel that children who understand how to add, subtract, multiply, and divide at an early age are extremely advanced in math and should be accelerated. This actually is what might be called *superficial math*. These children can rattle off math facts or do problems quickly, but they do not have a deep understanding of the subject. There is so much more to learn than just math facts or basic arithmetic. Rather than just accelerating students in math, it is highly recommended that students also be given the opportunity to explore topics in depth.

Before and Afterschool Activities

Before and afterschool clubs and competitions can provide exciting enrichment. If your elementary or middle school does not offer math clubs and competitions, can you find these opportunities elsewhere in your community? Sometimes local colleges have afterschool or Saturday programs for young people. If there are no such groups already organized, you may be willing to start one or find someone else with the expertise. You can approach school personnel to see if there is a way to do this. The sections below on Supplementary Materials From Publishers and Math Competitions are good places to obtain materials. Some of the math competitions actually provide formats for clubs, including teacher materials and problems on which the kids can work. Once your student is in high school, her abilities should be advanced enough that it is best to leave these enrichment possibilities to adults who have math degrees.

Supplementary Materials From Publishers

Often parents ask where they can get good materials to work with their kids on math at home. There are a number of publishers that primarily market to educators, but also are good resources for parents of elementary and middle school students. Look through their online catalogs and you will find all kinds of interesting materials. These publishers include:

- AIMS Education Foundation—http://www.aimsedu. org

  This publisher produces K–10 activity resource books and a magazine/newsletter. I especially like the *Historical Connections in Mathematics* books. These are geared to grades 6–12 and come in three volumes that connect history and mathematics. Each of three volumes explores the lives of 30 mathematicians. Ready-to-use activities are provided that help students "discover" the theories and work of each pioneer in the subject.

- Continental Mathematics League, Inc.—http://www.continentalmathematicsleague.com

  This actually is a competition, but you don't have to enter to benefit from this organization. Instead, you can buy books that contain some of the best math questions that are used in the competition. These books can be purchased for grades 2–3, 4–6, and 7–9. Each book contains individual problems that will really make your young person think. It is extremely helpful for students to talk through the different strategies used in solving the problems, as there often are many different possible approaches.

- Creative Publications—http://www.creativepublications.com

  This publisher includes a wide variety of books that use manipulatives and contain critical thinking activities.

- ETA/Cuisenaire—http://www.etacuisenaire.com

  This math catalog is filled with all kinds of wonderful products from a variety of publishers. There are basic manipulative materials, games, books, and posters. There are many books that use common items like dominoes, dice, and playing cards to help teach math. These provide inexpensive activities that will extend the math curriculum in exciting ways. Books using tessellations and paper folding provide enrichment in geometry and the power of patterns.

Distance Learning

A number of well-respected universities across the country offer multimedia, computer-based, distance-learning courses in math for gifted precollege students, and I expect more and more will be doing so in the future. Internet learning is constantly evolving. Some of the early classes that were offered by these institutions were not very compelling. They required a great deal of adult support and supervision, especially for elementary students. Distance learning techniques have improved and will continue to get better. Before you enroll your young person in one of these courses, make certain you ask a lot of questions, view sample lessons, and ask to communicate with parents of students who have tried the program. Students who are most successful with these programs are those who are able to stay motivated while working independently. (Be sure and look at the list of Resources for Distance Learning in Chapter 6.)

Math Competitions

Math competitions offer a forum to pit one's skills against the skills of others. They also offer opportunities to practice good problem-solving techniques. The adult coach of these competitions should have an excellent background in math. The competition may be headed by a math teacher or someone in the community, possibly a parent, who is confident in the subject.

One needs to plan well in advance to set up a mathematics competition. Just choosing the appropriate one in which to participate in is a challenge. Many of the sites below list sample problems, so you can get a taste of what each one involves. Although most competitions are for high school students, there are a handful at the middle school/junior high level, and just a few at elementary grade levels. When a range of grade levels is listed, there usually are competitions set up for just one or two grades at a time (i.e., separate tests for grades 3–4, 5–6, and 7–8). The competitions below appear in alphabetical order, not according to level of difficulty.

- American Regions Math League—http://www.arml.com

    The American Regions Math League is written for high school students, although some exceptional junior high students participate each year. The program involves almost 2,000 students and teachers from nearly every state. The competition consists of several events, which include a team round, a power question (in which a team solves proof-oriented questions), an individual round, two relay rounds (in which a contestant solves a problem and passes his or her answer to another team member, who uses this answer to solve another problem), and a super relay.

- The Harvard-MIT Mathematics Tournament—http://web.mit.edu/hmmt/www

    This is an annual math tournament for high school students, held at MIT and at Harvard in alternate years. Problems, solutions, and results from past HMMT contests are available at the Web site. Although most students enroll as a team, the competition also accepts students who enroll individually.

- The High School Mathematical Contest in Modeling (HiMCM)—http://www.comap.com/highschool/contests

  This contest for high school students is designed to improve mathematical problem-solving proficiency and writing skills. Teams of no more than four work on a real-world problem in a consecutive 36-hour period. The HiMCM Web site also has a large database of math problems.

- Mandelbrot—http://web.mandelbrot.org

  Two contests are offered at the high school level. The first is the Mandelbrot Competition, which adheres to a short-answer format and takes place in five rounds spread throughout the school year. The range of questions and topics is designed to engage students with only a modest background in problem solving while still stretching the best students in the country. The second contest is the Mandelbrot Team Play, which emphasizes mathematical writing skills and effective group work. This contest is held in three rounds during the winter months to help advanced students prepare for events such as the USAMO (see below).

- Math League—http://www.mathleague.com/contests.htm

  Math League offers contests for grades 4–8, high school students, and Algebra 1 students. Each contest can be completed in 30 minutes. Problems are grade appropriate.

- Math Olympiads—http://www.moems.org

  The goals of the Math Olympiads program are to stimulate enthusiasm and love for mathematics, introduce important concepts, teach major strategies, develop flexibility in solving problems, and foster creativity. School math clubs (grades 4–6 and 7–8) meet weekly for an hour. Students participate in five monthly contests, given between November and March in each participating school.

- The Mathematical Association of America: American Mathematics Competitions—http://www.unl.edu/amc

  The American Mathematics Competitions (AMC) are dedicated to the goal of strengthening the mathematical capabilities of our nation's youth by identifying, recognizing, and rewarding excellence in mathematics through a series of national contests for grades 8–12. A series of five contests and two international competitions are intended for everyone from the average student at a typical school who enjoys mathematics to the very best student at the most special school.

- MATHCOUNTS—http://mathcounts.org

  The MATHCOUNTS program provides schools with the structure and activities to hold regular meetings of a math club. Students enrolled in grades 6–8 are eligible to participate in MATHCOUNTS® competitions.

The competitions are organized at four levels: school, chapter (local), state, and national.

- United States of America Mathematical Olympiad (USAMO)—http://www.unl.edu/amc/e-exams/e8-usamo/usamo.shtml

  This contest provides a means of identifying and encouraging the most creative secondary mathematics students in the country. The USAMO is a 6-question, 2-day, 9-hour essay/proof examination. All problems can be solved with precalculus methods.

- USA Mathematical Talent Search—http://www.usamts.org

  This is a free mathematics competition open to all United States middle and high school students. Students have a full month to work out their solutions. Carefully written justifications are required for each problem. The problems range in difficulty from those within the reach of most high school students to challenging the best students in the nation. Students may use any materials—books, calculators, computers—but all the work must be their own. The USAMTS is run on the honor system—it is an individual contest, and its competitive role is secondary.

SCIENCE

The No Child Left Behind Act (2001) has caused both science and social studies to be placed on the back burner, especially in the early grades. Parents should do everything they can to expose children to these subjects through books, museums, nature centers, Web sites, and hands-on activities. Through exposure, kids will let you know their areas of interest.

Young children love to learn about animals, insects, and the world around them. Visit nature preserves, zoos, and streams or lakes. Spend time observing the environment with your child. Don't just notice the things that are obvious. Look up at the sky and get your noses down into the grass to see both the big and little worlds that often are overlooked. Take out the magnifying glass to observe up close. As you examine objects, smells, and the forces of nature, help your child discover patterns that occur and pose questions together. What is similar and different between these bugs or flowers? What do you think this animal eats or what are his natural enemies? How does the animal or insect protect itself? Where does our water come from? Posing questions will lead to finding answers through reading books or searching on the Internet. Your child will "lead" you in areas that interest him. The more you expose your young person to aspects of science, the greater the chance she will find an area she wants to pursue.

As students enter middle school and high school, more science courses are available, and some of these courses are taught at pretty high levels; however, teenagers with a strong interests and/or ability in science will want to pursue the field in more depth. With a little searching, opportunities for older students are available in advanced areas. A limited number of very capable high school students will need to find mentors to further their specialized studies. (Be sure to consult Chapter 6, which specifically talks about finding a mentor in science.)

Advanced Science Internet Resources

There are lots of wonderful Web sites where students can pursue their interest in science. Cogito (http://www.cogito.org) is one created by the Center for Talented Youth (CTY) at Johns Hopkins University. This site should be visited by anyone who has a strong interest in science. Although there is information for students of all ages, the primary emphasis is high school. News and features are presented on topics ranging from global warming and biostatistics, to cold fusion and bioethics. A variety of great resources are available, including book reviews; best of the Web guides; and listings and reviews of summer and distance-education programs, internships, and academic competitions.

Students who are members (by invitation only from Cogito Partners and Affiliates) also can participate in online interviews with experts in various fields and in discussion forums with other members. Membership also grants access to the Cogito.org virtual library where students can find a wide variety of research materials and a dedicated librarian.

In addition, Cogito.org publishes student-written work. Ideas must be submitted before sending actual drafts. Acceptable student submissions include full-length book and movie reviews, feature stories and articles, and essays.

A new wave in technology, known as Open Access, Open Educational Resources, or Open Course Ware, is allowing universities and scientists to share their lectures and expertise. Instructional videos are available for students of all ages—elementary through graduate school. Science is a big benefactor.

SciVee (http://www.scivee.tv) operates in partnership with the Public Library of Science (PLoS), the National Science Foundation (NSF), and the San Diego Supercomputer Center (SDSC). SciVee is a Web site that contains some material for elementary students and larger quantities of material for older students that is made available through scientists. Young people who are interested in careers in science will be fascinated by the various topics currently being studied. Just seeing what is going on at different universities may help students focus on their future objectives.

Examples of videos available at SciVee for younger students include *Dissections, Freezing by Boiling,* and *Where Does Water Go When It Rains?* There also is much information on highly sophisticated topics that will be appealing for able high school students.

Bio-Alive Life Science (http://bio-alive.com) is another open access Web site. Available here are video lectures and seminars, animations, tutorials and quizzes, virtual laboratories, video conferences, educational games, and videos of surgical procedures.

See the section in this chapter on technology for other sources of Web sites where open educational resources can be found.

Other science Internet sites worth looking at include:

- Hoagies' Kids and Teens Links—http://www.hoagiesgifted.org/links.htm

  This site contains a host of links under the categories of Science, Natural Science, Physics and Mechanics, and Space.
- National Aeronautics and Space Administration (NASA)—http://www.nasa.gov

  This is NASA's official Web site and has everything you ever wanted to know about space.
- Neuroscience for Kids—http://faculty.washington.edu/chudler/neurok.html

  Designed for students in elementary through high school, this Web site provides a wealth of information on the brain in fun, clear, easy-to-understand terms and illustrations. Not only is there great information, but there also are experiments, activities, questions and answers, other links and resources, and a place to sign up for a free newsletter.
- Society for Science & the Public—http://www.societyforscience.org

  This organization educates and informs students, parents, teachers, and the greater community about the evolving and influential world of science. It contains a comprehensive database of science, mathematics, and engineering enrichment programs for precollege students and teachers.

Science Fairs and Competitions

In many elementary, middle, and high schools, science fairs occur annually. These fairs offer gifted students a chance to explore areas of interest in depth. The fairs also provide opportunities for planning, discipline, and academic rigor. There is much information available on the Internet to help students and parents, including help in choosing a topic, tips, resources, and sample judging sheets. As a parent of a younger child, you may support your student by asking probing questions, helping to find resources, and advising; however, the real work needs to be done by the youngster.

PARENT RESOURCES: SCIENCE FAIRS

- All Science Fair Projects—http://www.all-science-fair-projects.com

  Here there are lists of topics for elementary, middle school, and high school science fair projects and a search tool that will help students find ideas. Also included are links to useful sites.

- Math Projects for Science Fairs—http://camel.math.ca/Education/mpsf

  Science fair ideas are included here for those with a very strong bent towards mathematics.

- Science Buddies—http://www.sciencebuddies.org

  The site includes science fair project ideas (including a wizard to walk students through the process of choosing a project), a project fair guide, resources, and a science fair blog.

- Science Fair Central—http://school.discoveryeducation.com/sciencefaircentral

    This site's student section includes a "soup to nuts" science fair handbook, project ideas, links and books, questions and answers, and tip sheets. For parents, there are tips on helping your young scientist.

- School Science Fairs Resource Page—http://www.cdli.ca/sciencefairs

    This site is designed to aid students in the most difficult aspect of their science fair experience—coming up with an idea.

- ScienceStuff.com—http://sciencefairproject.virtualave.net/judging_sheet.htm

    This is a sample science fair judging sheet to help the student and parent better understand how a project may be evaluated.

There are many science competitions for older students, some with extraordinary prizes, but most of them are only available if sponsored through one's school. The most successful students in these competitions almost always have professional mentors, often research specialists at universities.

PARENT RESOURCES: SCIENCE COMPETITIONS

- Siemens Competition in Math, Science, and Technology—http://www.siemens-foundation.org/en/competition.htm

    This competition promotes excellence by encouraging students to undertake individual or team research projects in science, mathematics, engineering, and technology or in combinations of these disciplines. Scholarships for winning projects range from $1,000 for regional finalists to $100,000 for national winners.

- Society for Science & the Public—http://www.societyforscience.org

    Here you will find information about the Intel Science Talent Search, one of the oldest and most prestigious science research competitions for high school seniors. There also is information about the Intel International Science and Engineering Fair, the world's largest international pre-college science competition for students in grades 9–12.

- Young Epidemiology Scholars Competition—http://www.collegeboard.com/yes

    The Young Epidemiology Scholars (YES) Competition for original student research is designed to inspire talented students to investigate the many behavioral, biological, environmental, and social factors that affect health and, based upon this knowledge, to identify ways to improve the health of the public.

- Young Naturalist Awards—http://www.amnh.org/nationalcenter/youngnaturalistawards

    This is a research-based essay contest for students in grades 7–12 that is sponsored by the American Museum of Natural History. Award winning essays can be read online.

Girls and Science

For the longest time there was a great concern about girls either being excluded from or not choosing to enter the field of science. It appears that some of that concern is shifting now.

In December 2007, girls walked away with top honors in both the individual and team categories of the Siemens Competition on Math, Science, and Technology, one of the nations' most prestigious student science contests (Siemens Foundation, 2007). Some of the winners included 16-year-old Isha Jain, a senior at Freedom High School in Bethlehem, PA, who was awarded a $100,000 scholarship for her studies of bone growth in zebra fish. The tail fins of the zebra fish grow in spurts, similar to the way child's bones do. Janelle Schlossberger and Amanda Marinoff, both 17-year-old seniors at Plainview-Old Bethpage John F. Kennedy High School in Plainview, NY, split a $100,000 scholarship for creating a molecule that helps block the reproduction of drug-resistant tuberculosis bacteria. And, Alicia Darnell, a 17-year-old senior at Pelham Memorial High School in Pelham, NY, won a $50,000, second-place award for research that identified genetic defects that could play a role in the development of Lou Gehrig's disease.

In 2007, 48% of the contestants and 11 of the 20 finalists were female (Siemens Foundation, 2007). It was the first year that girls outnumbered boys in the final round. Eighty percent of the competitors were from public high schools. One team of finalists consisted of homeschooled girls. Girls like Isha, Janelle, Amanda, and Alicia continue to excel in science. One resource for parents interested in encouraging their daughter's interest in science is Girls Go Tech (http://www.girlsgotech.org), a Web site and program sponsored by Girl Scouts of America to help support female students in their pursuit of science learning and careers.

SOCIAL STUDIES

The subject of social studies explores the relationship of people to each other and to their world. It draws upon many disciplines, including geography, history, economics, politics, anthropology, archaeology, law, philosophy, political science, psychology, religion, and sociology. Social studies easily integrates with all other disciplines and helps students become active and responsible citizens.

Geography

Peter was a second grader who was a whiz at geography. His father introduced him to the subject before the boy started elementary school, and he had been devouring it ever since. If you asked Peter to locate any place on the world map, he could point right to it. But, he wasn't just good at naming places. He could tell you the climate, the animals, and the vegetation of the area. If asked to reason why a certain event might take place in a specific country or city, he would pause and then begin his sentence very slowly with, "Let's see . . . " He would then take all of the information he knew about the location and reason very logically why that event might have taken place there. He might also add, "But I would also like to know . . . " Peter was a phenomenal reader. At second grade, he was reading at a 12th-grade level. This enabled him to do research easily. Peter definitely was gifted in geography.

I wonder how many other kids might show strong aptitudes in geography if they were just exposed to it. After all, a child can't get excited about something to which he has never been introduced. While most students in first or second grades are learning about their neighborhoods, Peter was exploring the world.

To encourage the study of geography, have lots of resources available at home, including maps, atlases, and globes. Sasha's family had a large, colorful world map hanging in their kitchen. If anyone in the family read about a place, they could look it up immediately. If a family member was doing a crossword puzzle and one of the questions pertained to geography, that person could find the answer on the map. Have maps for everything. If you live in a sports-oriented area, have maps of bike trails, hiking trails, ski slopes, and cross-country ski trails. Also interesting are topographical maps, relief maps, political maps, and weather maps. If you live in a big city, buy a map showing where all of the museums and parks are located. Each type of map has different symbols and information.

If you go to the zoo, get a map of the animal locations. If you go to a museum, pick up a map showing the layout of the exhibits. Have your child make a map of your house. Talk about the arrangement of the rooms and how the present locations function. Then have your child create a map of his ideal house. Have him explain why he placed the rooms where he did. Is it more functional that way or is it just more fun?

Use maps when studying history. Observe how borders change. Why do they change? How does geography influence where people settle? How does it affect where people move?

Discuss geography in relationship to current events. How does geography affect alliances and conflicts throughout the world? Why do the names of countries change?

Teach students how to read legends. Understand longitude and latitude and time zones. How does geography affect climate? Make this subject a part of everyday life both at home and at school.

Geography is so much more than names and locations. To help people gain a greater understanding of geography, the Joint Committee on Geographic Education of the National Council for Geographic Education (NCGE) and the Association of American Geographers (AAG) developed Five Themes of Geography. These themes give us relevant reasons to learn where everything is in the world and why it is important. The Web site also lists many activities to teach the five themes (see http://www.nationalgeographic.com/resources/ngo/education/themes.html). The themes are (National Geographic, n.d.):

- Location—Where are things located? Locations can be specific, such as coordinates of longitude and latitude, or general, such as a region.
- Place—What makes one place different from other places? Differences may include climate, physical features, or people and their traditions.
- Human-environment interaction—What are the relationships among people and places? How have people changed the environment and why?
- Movement—What are the patterns of movement of people, products, and information? This includes major

types of transportation used by people, an area's major exports and imports, and ways in which people communicate (move ideas).

- Regions—How can Earth be divided into regions for study? Regions can be defined by area, language, governments, religions, and vegetation (e.g., grassland, marshland, desert, or rainforest).

Parents should keep these themes in mind when talking with their children about geography. They also make great learning tools when traveling with children.

PARENT RESOURCES: GEOGRAPHY

- National Geographic—http://www.nationalgeographic.com

  There is a wealth of geographic information at this Web site, including lots of information and fun activities for the younger set and suggestions for parents.
- GeoBee Challenge—http://www.nationalgeographic.com/geobee

  The National Geographic Bee is a competition open to students in grades 4–8. This Web site offers information about registering for the competition and also study materials and daily questions that are valuable for all students.

History

The study of history provides a framework for understanding current events. There are many venues for exploring this subject including specialty reading materials, research and writing, competitions, traditional museums, and living museums.

Reading Materials

There are some great history magazines available for kids beginning at age 9. Well-researched articles, magnificent photos, and hands-on activities make learning about our world fun and engaging. At http://www.cobblestonepub.com/mags_socialstudies.html, you will find several such magazines, including:

- *Calliope*—World history including dramatic tales, high-interest art from the world's leading museums, timelines, and maps.
- *Cobblestone*—American history through true stories and dramatic photographs.
- *Dig*—Archaeologists and historians explore the mysteries of ancient civilizations. Read about the cultural, scientific, and architectural accomplishments of societies from all corners of the world.

Many students (and adults) dislike history because it seems like an endless memorization of meaningless names, dates, and battles. History really comes alive when one sees the interesting interactions and the idiosyncrasies of people and places.

Joy Hakim, a former teacher and newspaper woman, decided to make history come alive in the most interesting way for students as young as age 8. She wrote the 10-volume, highly illustrated series *A History of US* (2002a). These books, which are well-researched and historically accurate, contain stories that grab young people. Hakim (2002b) also wrote *Freedom: A History of US*, a one-volume book written as a companion to a 16-part PBS miniseries, which is now available on video and DVD. This television series features the voices of Paul Newman, Glenn Close, Robin Williams, Tom Hanks, Matthew Broderick, and Morgan Freeman, among others.

Some of these materials (especially the 10-volume series) are expensive. If your child's school or local library does not carry them, encourage them to do so.

Reading and studying original documents is still another way to learn about history. There are some great resources for finding original documents online, including The Library of Congress (http://www.loc.gov) where much of the library has been digitized. There also is a special section of this Web site for kids and families.

RESEARCH AND WRITING

When I took my first history course in college, the president of the university (a history buff himself) spoke to our class and encouraged us to submit our papers to various journals for publication. Being rather inexperienced, it had never occurred to me to submit anything I had ever written to anyone for publication. In my mind, I was just a student and couldn't imagine anyone being interested in what I wrote.

Now it is possible not only for serious college students to publish their work, but for serious high school history students to publish the papers that they have researched. *The Concord Review* (http://www.tcr.org) gives young people this opportunity.

The Concord Review is the only quarterly journal in the world to publish the academic expository research papers of secondary history students. Papers may be written on any historical topic, ancient or modern, foreign or domestic, and may be submitted in two categories: short (1,500–2,500 words) and long (4,000–6,000 words).

Many young authors have sent reprints of their papers along with their college application materials. Their research has helped them to gain admission to some of the nation's (and world's) best universities.

Students also can use *The Concord Review* to see examples of good historical writing. What a wonderful opportunity for students to see the work of age peers who have taken their work seriously. Included on *The Concord Review* Web site are more than 60 sample essays for both students and teachers to view so they can get an idea of the quality of work accepted.

At this site, you also will find information about The National Writing Board, an independent assessment service for the academic writing of high school students of history. Each submission is assessed by two readers who know nothing about the author. These readers spend more than 3 hours on each paper. Three-page evaluations, with scores and comments are then sent at the request of the authors to Deans of Admissions at the colleges to which they apply.

COMPETITIONS

National History Day (http://www.nationalhistoryday.org) is a competition for students in grades 6–12. Participants engage in discovery and interpretation of historical topics related to an annual theme. Students hone their talents and produce creative and scholarly projects in the form of exhibits, documentaries, historical papers, performances, or Web sites. After a series of district and state contests, the program culminates with a national competition at the University of Maryland in College Park each June.

TRADITIONAL AND LIVING MUSEUMS

Whether in your own hometown or on a family vacation, traditional and living history museums are great places to visit. In addition to visiting permanent exhibits, consider a return for special exhibits at your local history museum. When traveling, look for living museums, where historical communities from the past are reconstructed and docents don historical dress and assume roles of the past, speaking in the character of the period.

Economics

Economics describes the production, distribution, and consumption of goods and services and their financial considerations. Specialty materials and programs in this area are more limited.

There are a number of ways for students to learn about investing and the stock market, all of which are instructional, entertaining, and competitive.

- The Stock Market Game™ (http://smgww.org)—This is an Internet-based experience at school that gives students in grades 4–12 the chance to invest a hypothetical $100,000 to create the best-performing portfolio using a live trading simulation. Students work together in teams, practicing leadership, organization, negotiation, and cooperation as they compete for the top spot.
- Bull Market (Great Canadian Game Company Inc.)—This is a board game for ages 12 to adult where players try to make the most money by trading stocks. They learn about stock splits, money management, bookkeeping, IPO's, and more. They attempt to accumulate stock at low prices with the anticipation that their stocks will skyrocket.
- Stock Market Tycoon (Vida Games LLC)—This board game is recommended for ages 8 to adult. Become the first investor to earn more than $1 million, and attempt to close the market. But, make sure your stocks are up when you do or the real tycoon will emerge and retire to the tropical island of his or her choice.

The National Economics Challenge (http://economicschallenge. ncee.net) is a competition that takes place in 35 different states. There are two different divisions: one for high school students taking Advanced Placement, International Baccalaureate, honors, college-level, or two-semester classes; the other for students enrolled in all other general or one-semester economics classes. There are monetary prizes for both students and teachers.

FOREIGN LANGUAGE

Some time ago, I had an opportunity to visit an American family who was living and working in a remote area of South America. I was very impressed with their 5-year-old daughter who spoke three languages fluently: English, Spanish, and Quechua (the indigenous language of the Andean region). She actually was more fluent than her parents in Quechua and sometimes acted as a translator for them. No one had made an effort to teach her these languages, but because she was exposed to each on a daily basis at such an early age, she picked them up on her own. She moved with ease between the languages, quickly ascertaining who would understand which one.

Students in many other parts of the world begin studying other languages in elementary school and often are proficient in several by the time they reach secondary school. In the United States, we often delay this study until middle or high school. Are we losing an opportunity by doing so?

Reasons for beginning foreign language study at an early age include the following:

- Students are able to develop a greater proficiency, as they have more years to develop skills.
- Children develop global attitudes through intercultural awareness.
- Language learning skills transfer from one language learning experience to another. Knowledge of one foreign language facilitates the study of a second foreign language.

Occasionally foreign languages are offered in elementary schools either during the school day or in classes before or after school. You also may be able to find classes offered elsewhere in your community.

Another great way to learn or improve language skills is to participate in a language immersion camp, where only the specific foreign language is spoken. You can do an Internet search for language immersion camps in your area to see if one is available.

One camp that I have heard great things about is the Concordia Language Villages in northern Minnesota (http://clvweb. cord.edu/prweb). At the Concordia Language Villages, they teach 14 languages (including Chinese, Finnish, Arabic, Korean, and Russian) and have sessions ranging from one weekend to 4 weeks for students 7–18 years of age. All levels, from beginner through advanced, are welcome. Day camps are available at several locations in Minnesota for children 4–8 years of age to learn languages such as Norwegian, German, and Spanish. There are even family weeks. Scholarships and financial aid are available to participants. In fact, nearly 15% of the villagers receive scholarships.

For students who want to learn a foreign language independently or supplement classes they are taking in school, check out podcasts. If you go to iTunes (http://www.apple.com/itunes) and download the free iTunes software, you can do a search at the iTunes store and subscribe to free podcasts for just about any language you can imagine. Many of these providers also offer PDF files of written materials to support the lessons. By using the printed materials, students can see the printed word, plus follow up with written exercises.

As technology continues to improve, it makes subjects like learning another language incredibly interactive and fun. With LiveMocha (http://www.livemocha.com), one can learn a new language, progressing at his own pace with both visuals and audio. As of this writing, the Web site is free. Members have the opportunity to communicate with real native speakers by writing, talking together, and even using a Webcam. Presently, viewers can learn Chinese, French, German, Hindi, Italian, Japanese, Portuguese, Russian, and Spanish. English also is offered for non-English speakers.

FINE ARTS

Exposing young people to all types of culture (music, art, dance, theater, architecture, and so forth) is part of a well-rounded education. However, only a small percentage of students truly can be considered gifted in these areas. Gifted students will show sustained interest and self-direction and can best be assessed by experts in the area of interest. Although many people show strong talents from early ages, they may not maintain their interest. In fact, there are people who have eventually proven to be the most gifted who have not produced at a high level until they were adults.

In some cities, magnet or specialty schools are available for students who are talented in these areas.

Music

Adam's parents used to laugh about him because he would sing himself to sleep long before he could talk. After he was put down for a nap, visitors would say, "What's he doing?" He mother replied that she always rocked and sang their first child to sleep, but she didn't have as much time with Adam, so she just taught him to sing himself to sleep.

When he was still very little, he would sit for long periods of time listening to and singing with the music. His parents had lots of music that he played over and over again.

When Adam was 3, his grandmother gave the family the piano that his mother played as a child. Adam begged to learn. His mom started teaching him and there was no stopping him after that. Adam eventually majored in piano in college. Does that make him gifted? His parents did understand one thing. They could not expect the public schools to meet his needs in music as he was growing up. He was too advanced. How much should we realistically expect public schools to do for students who are very capable in music or art?

Adam's parents never even considered that he should be taught piano in school. Instead, they hired the best private teachers they could afford. As Adam approached middle school, he spent part of his summer vacations at a music camp where the kids practiced 5 hours a day and had lots of private lessons and performance opportunities. He absolutely loved it. It was the first time he had ever met others who shared his interest so passionately. The family was fortunate, because they could afford the private lessons and the camp. It is much more difficult for those who are not in that position. For families who cannot afford lessons for children with promise, there are organizations, such as The MusicLink Foundation (http://www.musiclinkfoundation. org), which may be able to help.

Art

What about art? How can we, as adults, judge the artistic ability of young people—or should we be judging it at all? Does the creation of realistic renditions when a child is young indicate that she has an artistic bent or is she just copying what she sees in her environment? What does it mean to be a gifted artist?

Jonathan Fineberg, a professor of art history at University of Illinois, was the curator of an exhibition of works by Pablo Picasso, Paul Klee, and other famous artists that were created when they were very young. Fineberg hung their works alongside dozens of drawings and paintings by modern kids, ages 4 and up. Be sure to listen to the NPR interview with Fineberg by Michele Norris at *"When We Were Young": Art That's Not Child's Play* (http:// www.npr.org/templates/story/story.php?storyId=5529588). There are examples of the early work of both artists who went on to be famous and art from young children today. The interview is excellent. Fineberg points out indicators of early gifted ability in art. The indicators are not stark realism, but a sense of character and humor in art, visual nuances, interesting composition, and an uninhibited freshness.

Some things to remember when looking at young artists are:

- The demonstration or nondemonstration of artistic ability at a young age is not necessarily a predictor of one's abilities as an adult. Many famous artists did not produce anything until they were older.

- Those with real talent often are obsessed with their artistic creations. It's difficult for them to stop and do something else. These children can't get their ideas down fast enough. They don't need stimulation.

- Adults need to be careful not to impose their values and aspirations on a child and her artwork. The gifted child can be very expressive but only if the experience motivating her is personally meaningful. Such a child may not respond well to classroom activities where the teacher sets the topic.

- Adults need to be careful not to give too many instructions to a child.

- Parents must be careful not to push a child into a place that the child doesn't want to be, such as showing off or exhibiting his work or selling it. Parents can sometimes put too much of their own ambition into the child.

Don't be concerned if, as a parent, you know very little about art. Some of the greatest artists also had mothers or fathers who knew very little about the subject. Visit art galleries with your children and help them become familiar with the art sections of the library. Enjoy your child's creativity but don't make a great fuss over it.

Recommendations to parents also include:
- Buy lots of cheap paper so you won't feel it is being wasted.
- Display the work of all of your children—not just the one best at art.
- Teach your child to respect the work of others.
- Don't correct wrong proportions.
- Don't encourage competitiveness in art.
- Send your child to art classes if she is interested.
- Allow experimentation.

Jan Brett is a popular author/illustrator of children's books. She is especially fond of drawing animals. Jan Brett's videos (http://janbrett.com/video/video_main_page.htm) easily could be used at school, at home, or through a homeschooling experience to encourage artistic talent.

From the time Brett was in kindergarten, she knew she wanted to be an illustrator of children's books. The videos include interviews that share how this talented lady became interested in drawing, and the events in her youth that inspired her. She also talks about how she gets the ideas for the books she publishes now.

In addition to the interviews, there are more than a dozen videos where Brett shows how to draw various animals and objects, breaking down the process into small, easy-to-follow steps. She includes a dolphin, rhinoceros, creature of the deep, lion, baby polar bear, hedgehog, chick, African okapi, bunny, elephant, horse, and Siberian husky.

This Web site is an excellent resource for students who want to do an in-depth study on a children's author/illustrator. It also could serve as an inspiration for those who would someday like to publish their own work. After watching the videos, students may want to create their own illustrated books for fun.

Other Fine Arts

Just a few of the many other disciplines under the umbrella of fine arts are dance, theater, architecture, photography, cinematography. Look for opportunities at summer experiences (see Chapter 4), enrichment classes near your home, and community and professional theater (young people may be able to both be a member of the audience and, in some cases be part of the cast). Find tutors or mentors, visit museums and galleries, go on tours of architectural structures and the backstage areas of performance venues.

TECHNOLOGY

It was not many years ago when I heard many adults (teachers and parents) complain about the "imposition of technology" on society. They stressed that they simply didn't have the time to learn about it. They were too busy doing things that were more important.

Think of how technology has changed our lives in recent years. We have grown to love (and hate) computers with word processing, online bill paying, shopping, and financial management. Computers now can be integrated with televisions and music systems. They are used to remotely monitor activity at home and turn on and off various appliances. We have cell phones, text messaging, iPods, Blackberries, Bluetooth wireless devices—the list goes on. These do not feel like new technologies to young people, however. Today's young people were born into this new age era and these innovations are a completely normal part of their lives. Teachers often face students who know more about the digital landscape than the older generation.

Adults no longer have the luxury of not learning about and accepting technology, because it has become integrated into society and the ways people learn. Yes, it may have its drawbacks, but it also opens possibilities that most of us had never considered. It is exciting to think that this is all still in its infancy. As we look back in history, we see the tremendous changes that occurred during movements such as the Industrial Revolution. Right now, we are living history, because we are witnessing the Technology Revolution. Although we've seen a lot of technological changes in society over the last decade or so, these changes are increasing exponentially with no end in sight. Gifted students are one of the groups that can benefit from this technological revolution.

I recently was in another city, where I met a number of students attending college and graduate school. Whenever I meet bright, young people, I am fascinated to learn about the jobs they have or are planning to have. Many of the job opportunities today are vastly different from the jobs that were available when I was young. For gifted students, career opportunities also may involve much higher levels of education. We need to be careful that we are preparing young people for this changing world.

The greatest change I see is the application of technology and the jobs this is creating. For instance, I met several people on my trip who are working on doctoral degrees that combine artificial intelligence and psychology. They are trying to figure out how to relate the thought process of the brain to technology. So far, they are applying this knowledge to training simulations for the military and private companies, but they also predict that the field will eventually infiltrate our basic education system. Of course, no one knows what this will look like yet, but it has the potential to truly individualize education according to each student's strengths, needs, and interests (a philosophy we have always encouraged in gifted education).

Another graduate student is combining his interests of technology and psychology to find applications that will aid people with health problems. What is it that very ill people need to improve their lives and how can we create technological systems to help them?

Another major change that is taking place, largely because of technological advances, is the globalization of jobs. I asked the young people I met where they planned to live and work. They saw the world as their platter. They might live and work almost anywhere in the world or they might choose one place to live and telecommute to other countries. In my parents' generation, a person usually got a job close to home and kept that job for the duration of his career. (I specifically said "his career," because it was primarily men who worked at that time.) In my generation, job opportunities began to open up for women and people often considered moving away from their hometowns. In fact, some people moved numerous times. With the present generation, there are newly invented jobs, young people think globally about where they might live, and it is predicted that they will not only change positions numerous times, but actually change careers a number of times.

We need to seriously consider if our methods for teaching kids are keeping up with our changing society. Are we giving students the skills they will need to meet the challenges of change—especially in regards to technology and globalization? Are we teaching them skills of flexibility and supplying them with a comfort for change so that they will be prepared for jobs of the future that haven't yet been created?

Differentiating curriculum for a wide variety of student abilities always has been a challenge. Computers are becoming an increasingly successful tool for accomplishing this. Students are now able to explore content in depth using the Internet. They have access to original documents, virtual museums, videos, university lectures, and online classes. These resources work especially well with highly motivated, independent learners who have special areas of interest. (For more information on distance learning, see Chapter 6.)

Computer and other technology games often get a bad rap, but there are many good programs out there that really hone in on problem-solving skills. Games like the *SimCity*® series and

Roller Coaster Tycoon® give kids interactive cognitive workouts. At every point one has to make decisions. Kids have to think about patterns, long-term goals, and resources. Then they need to make decisions, get feedback from the game, and use that to readjust their decisions. Game players learn about measured risk taking, have an amazing ability to multitask, and develop leadership skills. Games like *Brain Age* (Nintendo DS) provide simple, fun, even competitive mental exercise. This game is designed to give your brain a workout by solving simple math problems, counting currency, drawing pictures on the Nintendo DS touch screen, and unscrambling letters.

Computer games and simulations are becoming more and more refined as they are used as teaching tools in schools, businesses, and the military. Open Educational Resources (OER) are educational materials and resources offered freely and openly on the Internet for educators, students, and independent learners. The resources include class lectures, notes, conference presentations, and more. This material is especially appropriate for advanced high school students and can supplement almost any area of interest. In the past, one would have had to enroll in a class at a prestigious university or have a connection with a content specialist to have access to this information. The following are OER opportunities:

- Caltech Today—http://today.caltech.edu/theater
  Streaming video of programs at Caltech from 1999 to the present on science, technology, and social culture are available.

- Duke University Multimedia Classroom Video Archives—http://www.math.duke.edu/computing/broadcast.html

  This site contains all recorded video lectures produced in the Duke University Mathematics Department Multimedia Classroom.
- Free Video Lectures—http://freevideolectures.com

  This is a comprehensive site providing video lectures, lessons, audio lectures, podcasts, free online classes, courses, interactive online tutorials, and text materials like ebooks and lecture notes.
- Law School Video Lectures—http://jurist.law.pitt.edu/live.htm

  Webcasts of major law school lectures, conferences, panels, debates, and special events can be found here.
- MIT OpenCourseWare: Highlights for High School—http://ocw.mit.edu/OcwWeb/hs/home/home/index.htm

  This guide to MIT courses is selected specifically to help high school students prepare for AP exams, learn more about the skills and concepts they learn in school, and get a glimpse of what they'll study in college.
- OER Commons—http://www.oercommons.org

  At this site, you will find a vast collection of free online courses and other information. You can search by subject area or by grade level. A number of video segments from programs such as NOVA are available to watch online. Sample learning materials range from building a house for a teddy bear, to a 5-day view of the jet stream, to algebra, to 20th-century art.

- Princeton University Lectures—http://www.princeton.edu/WebMedia/lectures

  Included here are lectures from the Princeton Environmental Institute, Public Lecture Series, the James Madison Program in American Ideals and Institutions, and others. Sample titles are "Exploration of the Great Rivers of Africa," "Escher and the Droste Effect," and "The Legacy of John Adams."

- University of California at Berkeley—http://video.google.com/ucberkeley.html

  Videos include course lectures, readings, and symposiums in a variety of subjects.

Even some professors have been amazed at the number of people who are watching university lectures on the Internet now. Viewers come from a wide age range: Some are elementary school children, many are high school students, and others are adults who want to learn for a myriad of reasons.

General online video and audio capabilities are becoming more sophisticated and finding more educational applications. Some of the many samples of these can be found at the following sites:

- iTunes—http://www.apple.com/itunes

  You can download iTunes software for free. Once you have downloaded it, you will have access to podcasts on a wide variety of topics. You can either listen to these on your computer or you can move them over to your MP3 player. You can listen to anything from "Sesame Street" to Spanish lessons.

- PBS—http://www.pbs.org

  Search for either podcasts or videos and you will find a host of materials you can download on a wide variety of topics.

- YouTube—http://www.youtube.com

  This site has many good videos on every subject imaginable, but it needs parental screening for the younger set. For early learners, try searching for animals like polar bears or lions or the name of a specific music piece.

Gifted children often are interested in a wide variety of topics—many that would not normally be taught in school. Virtual museums allow students to pursue these topics by "visiting" collections around the world. Some museums housed online include:

- The Museum of Online Museums—http://www.coudal.com/moom

  This site provides links to online collections and exhibits covering a vast array of subjects, from classical art, to architecture, to mundane collectible objects. Links include MoMA (The Museum of Modern Art), The Smithsonian, a collection of advertisements printed in U.S. and Canadian newspapers and magazines between 1911 and 1955, and a museum of chocolate wrappers.

- Art and Museums Online—http://mason.g
  ~montecin/museum.htm

    Among many others, you will find links here to The
    Getty, The Guggenheim, The Library of Congress, and
    also to digital art.
- The Aviation History Online Museum—http://www.
  aviation-history.com

    This is a specialty site that has great pictures and
    history of all aspects of aviation.

Whatever the subject at hand, with today's quickly evolving
technologies, you're sure to find a valuable source of learning
through a simple Internet search.

THINKING SKILLS

One characteristic that can differentiate a bright person from
a truly gifted person is the way in which he thinks. A gifted
child looks at the world in a different way than most people.
There are ways that parents can encourage these attributes in
their kids at home by understanding and practicing them in
everyday conversations.

Metacognition

Metacognition is the analysis of one's own thinking process
or thinking about one's thinking. A great deal can be learned
about kids by just sitting down and probing. Once you start

talking with your child about his thinking, he will begin to understand his own mental processes and be able to apply the same strategies to other situations. Start when you see that your son is not getting along with his best friend or when your daughter is having a difficult time making a decision. Some statements and questions that you might use are:

- Think out loud for me.
- Tell me about the strategies you are using.
- Tell me more about why you did that.
- What are some things you will have to think about before beginning this?
- When did you start having trouble?
- What was it that confused you?
- Is this problem like any other problem you have experienced?
- Is there another way of looking at this?
- How did you develop that idea?

One day I was working with a class on some difficult math problems. After giving the students time to work individually on the problem, they still struggled. I suggested that we stop and share some of the strategies that students were using and how they were thinking about the problem. One rather quiet boy began explaining his thinking. Suddenly several others blurted out, "That will never work!" (I didn't think it would work either.) Instead of cutting the boy off, I told the others to be polite and hear him out. As he explained his thinking, the correct solution slowly emerged. Yes, he had approached the dilemma in an unusual way, but it yielded the correct answer. There often are many different interesting ways to approach a problem rather than only one right way. That makes learning interesting and exciting.

It will help your children if you model your own metacognition. When beset with a task, talk out loud and state how you will approach the task. Say if it reminds you of something you have done before. Anticipate what information or tools you will need to accomplish the task. When something isn't working, stop and talk out loud. What might be a different strategy you could try? "Last night I got to bed too late and today I was tired. I think I should start my chores earlier tonight and set an absolute time when I will call it a day."

Christopher was about to read *War and Peace*. He knew that it would be difficult to keep the multitude of characters straight in the book. He wondered how he could manage this, and he thought through the possibilities. He could take notes as he went along, but that would be cumbersome. He could go through the book and highlight the names as he read and write notes in the margin. In the end, he decided to turn to the Internet, find a list of characters with one-sentence summaries and print it out. That would be his reference point when the characters became confusing. Christopher used metacognition to help him figure out a solution to his problem.

Rather than focusing on judging, focus on thinking strategies: what works and what doesn't work. Don't tell the kids what they should do; instead, help them figure out strategies for figuring out resolutions themselves. When students learn tacognition, they become more confident. They learn roaches to take. By helping them with this when they ig, you will help them better understand their choices in the future.

Critical Thinking

Students should be taught to think logically and analytically and not accept information as fact just because someone tells them it is so. We also want them to go beyond the memorization of facts and be able to examine, evaluate, and apply what they learn to their own lives. The ability to use one's mind critically helps a person to make thoughtful decisions about schoolwork, friends, politics, and directions to be taken in life.

Although the development of critical thinking skills is vital for all young people, it especially is important for gifted students. Students need to develop the ability to:

- evaluate information and opinions in a systematic, purposeful, efficient manner;
- solve complex problems;
- generate multiple (or creative) solutions to a problem;
- draw inferences;
- synthesize and integrate information;
- distinguish between fact and opinion;
- predict potential outcomes; and
- evaluate the quality of one's own thinking.

With very young children, start simple.

- Help children to evaluate their own work and decisions rather than just relying on adult comments. How do you feel about the way you worked on that project or solved that problem? What are the things you think you did well? What would you do differently next time?

- Help children to be good decision-makers. Give them many opportunities to practice. You have $5. What would you spend it on? Why? When confronted with a problem, help them to look at many different possible solutions, looking beyond the obvious. Guide them to select the most promising choices and consider the pros and cons of each. They then can select the decision they think is the best, supporting it with important reasons.

- Help children to look for patterns and purposes both tangible and intangible. What are the patterns in the spider web? What are the different patterns in our family's behavior?

- Help children connect subjects. After learning about the social life of bees or insects, ask your child, "How is a beehive like a city? How is it different?"

By teaching children critical thinking skills, you will help them to feel confident in themselves and you will prepare them to make good decisions as they grow.

We all have problems we'd like to solve. Some people aren't very good at math. Some people have nosy neighbors. Some people go to bed hungry at night. No matter how small or how big the problems are, we'd like to solve them. It's hard to solve a problem, though, unless we understand the problem very well. Who is involved in the problem? What is the problem? When and where does the problem occur? Why does the problem happen? How does it occur? The first step in successful problem solving is defining and describing the problem.

This is just one type of thinking fostered by Future Problem Solving Program International (FPSP; http://www.fpsp.org). The program (for students in grades 4–12) stimulates critical and creative thinking skills and encourages young people to develop visions for the future through both individual and team activities. It nurtures global awareness not only through choice of topics, but by knowing that the same problems are being studied by more than 250,000 students annually, including those from Australia, Canada, Hong Kong, Korea, Malaysia, New Zealand, Russia, and the United States.

You may want to consider instituting a program such as Future Problem Solving Program International at your school to support critical and creative thinking skills and encourage students to develop a vision for the future. Both competitive and noncompetitive activities are offered and even if your student never participates in the formal program, the organization's Web site contains good instructional materials for creative and critical thinking. Materials include both written offerings avail. purchase and also links to other Web sites.

Through FPSP, students learn to formulate and attack complex, ambiguous problems; analyze and better understand material; improve in oral and written communication; and work together in a team. Descriptions of current topics for FPSP are at the organization's Web site, so you can get a flavor of the range of real-world themes.

One publisher, Foundation for Critical Thinking (http://www.criticalthinking.org), specializes in materials to teach critical thinking skills. In addition to having materials for purchase, there are quite a few valuable articles available online at no cost. Materials are available for elementary school through adult.

According to Michael Tabachnick, professor of physics at Delaware Valley College in Doylestown, PA, who teaches a course in critical thinking,

> The easiest way to encourage critical thinking is to force [students] to question everything . . . Question me, question their parents, their pastor, everything. It doesn't mean you can't believe, but you must question. Is it true? Is it opinion? Is it justified by fact? . . . Students eventually learn to analyze. Some will do it better than others, but you can always get them to at least question. (Strauss, 2008, p. 2)

Seeing Patterns

Being able to conceptualize the repetition of patterns in life is a very helpful skill. For instance, Dr. Williams had a wonderful way of explaining things. He often needed to describe how the parts of the body worked and what happened when those parts did not work properly. Frequently he compared the systems of the body to common machinery or household systems. He helped his patients understand their illnesses by making connections to objects and experiences that were already familiar to them.

Children also learn best when they relate new information to things and ideas that are familiar. We can encourage them with this by helping them look at the world in terms of patterns:

- Rather than have kids just memorize math facts, show them the patterns of numbers. This will make the memorization much easier (e.g., the multiples of 5 are the same as counting up by 5 over and over again).

- Rather than learn a lot of historical facts—dates, names, battles—teach the concept of cause and effect. Then the dates, names, and battles will fall into place (e.g., Why did Germany begin its aggressive tactics preceding WWII? Are there similarities or differences preceding other world conflicts?).

- When studying literature, instead of checking only for comprehension, discuss the theme in relation to responsibility, or conflict, or survival (e.g., What does the story of *Goldilocks and the Three Bears* tell us about respecting the property of others? Have you ever had problems deciding when it is OK to use someone else's things? What were some of the personality characteristics of the third pig in *The Three Little Pigs* that enabled him to survive?).

Over time, the complexity of questions should increase. When having family discussions or helping young people work on school assignments, ask questions such as, "What evidence do you have . . . ?" or "How do you know that's true?" or "What do you think would happen if . . . ?" or "If that is true, then what might happen if . . . ?" If your child is researching a topic, ask questions such as, "How can you tell if it is a reputable source?" "How can a variety of sources help to paint a broader picture?" "How would you justify using this source?"

Critical thinking is essential to higher level thinking. It is one element that differentiates gifted kids from those who are not gifted.

CONCLUSION

Whether your young person has strengths across the board or only in one or two areas, you will want to support him in every way possible. Although I've provided many suggestions of ways to do this, I have offered only the tip of the iceberg. Use your imagination and let your student's interests guide you. Don't be surprised if her interests and strengths take you in an entirely different direction than you ever expected to go. That's part of the excitement of parenthood.

8

SOME UNIQUE GROUPS

IFTED children come in all shapes and sizes. Each subgroup of giftedness has its own unique characteristics and needs.

YOUNG CHILDREN

Although we may feel that it is important to identify a child's abilities at an early age, parents also need to be careful not to "wish" their children into giftedness.

One should not jump to conclusions about the perceived abilities that a child has and how those skills will be applied to the rest of his life. Some parents of very young children (perhaps just a year or two old) list all of the skills their young person has and enthusiastically declare that the child is gifted or even a genius. The expectation is that the child will continue to perform at this accelerated level for the rest of her life. When the child is still a toddler, the parents already are imagining that she will have her choice of any college she wants to attend and most likely be enrolled at an early age. Parents may even imagine that the preschooler eventually will save humanity through medical research, implement important social changes in the world, or become a famous musician. Why, one might ask, are the parents putting themselves and their child through this? Think of the possible scenarios that they are setting up for failure. If the child doesn't continue to perform, whose fault will it be? The parents'? The child's? The school's? Think of the pressure that will be felt by the child to always be a top performer.

Please don't misunderstand me. I am not suggesting that a child's strengths should be ignored. But, at the same time, don't assume that your child is operating at a level far above his age peers or that he will always perform at a very high level. You may not be qualified to properly assess your child's abilities. Let others who have experience working with many young people make that determination. You also need to know that it is not a common practice to formally assess the intellectual abilities of children at a very young age.

Meanwhile, let your young person enjoy her childhood and not feel pressured with expectations to change the world. Offer her a solid base of a loving family. Expose her to a wide variety of experiences and definitely support her interests. But please, don't burden her with the expectation that she always will be the shining star of academics, the arts, or sports.

When children see priorities of performance belonging to the parents and not to themselves, they do what comes naturally: they either find a way to resist, however illogical it may seem to the parents, or they strive extra hard to win their parents' approval, even at their own expense. Meeting the needs of one's child without imposing unreasonable pressure or transferring one's own dreams onto him does not mean we cease to have expectations for the child. We simply put those expectations into a framework that respects the child's needs as much as it respects the child's abilities.

There are several schools of thought on young, precocious children. Some believe that it is very important to identify a child at a very early age. If the child is not identified, she will be deprived of reaching her "potential." Some believe that a child may just appear to be gifted because he has been exposed to many experiences at an early age. Other children will eventually catch up to him. Still others believe that a child may be going through a developmental spurt when young, but this growth will slow down as she gets older. You will find opinions of experts to support each of these schools of thought.

When reading information about very young children, you often will find lists, such as "what to look for in a potentially gifted toddler." It is important to note the word *potentially*. Children who exhibit these characteristics may or may not be eventually identified as gifted. Possible traits that may, however, turn out to be indicators later on are:

- large vocabulary;
- long attention span;
- fast absorption of knowledge;
- deep understanding of questions and answers from adults;
- early walking or talking;

- early interest in the alphabet and/or numbers;
- ability to complete puzzles intended for older children;
- an advanced sense of humor;
- intolerance of something perceived to be unfair;
- need to organize, sort, arrange, and classify; and
- understanding of cause and effect and inferences.

No matter what you think your child's abilities are, expose her to a wide variety of experiences in a playful manner and support her interests. If your young person likes books, go to the library often and read lots of books together. If he expresses an interest in a particular subject, provide the necessary materials to support that interest.

There often is uneven development (or asynchrony) within a child—especially a young child (e.g., Sarah may be a whiz kid in math, but have very poor fine motor coordination). Frequently, these discrepancies even out over the years. In the first years of school, however, parents must understand that this is not unusual and that it is not initially a reason for concern.

UNDERACHIEVERS

There is nothing as frustrating as having a child who you know is very bright, yet does not perform. An underachiever is someone whose school performance does not match his high intellectual ability. Although many causes and strategies have been offered for resolving the problem, it is not a dilemma with a "cookie cutter" solution. Worse, it may not have any solution. But remember, while there are students who do incredibly well all the way through school and then fall flat on their faces, there are also kids who underachieve all the way through school and then do remarkably well once they are finished with their formal education.

Some of the reasons that have been given for underachievement include a dysfunctional family situation, internal pressures, lack of personal skills, undetected learning disabilities, or inappropriate school match.

Students are strongly impacted by their families. For reasons we don't fully understand, some youngsters will step beyond the difficulties at home and use learning positively as an escape or as something over which they can have control. More often, if a strong base is not offered at home, a child cannot get beyond those difficulties. If basic physical and psychological needs are not met, learning often is not considered important. Therefore, parents must carefully scrutinize their own parenting styles. Often we equate underachievers with "bad" families. We justify the fact that these students do poorly in school because they receive no support at home. This may be true in some cases, but there are many underachieving children who come from the best of homes. They have parents who care deeply about them, are hard workers themselves, and are involved in the schools.

Underachievement also may be caused by internal pressures such as perfectionism, supersensitivity, or a deficiency in social skills. Here, it may be helpful to employ the aid of a psychologist to help. Underachievement may be caused by a personal characteristic such as low self-motivation, low self-regulation (the ability to monitor, evaluate, and react appropriately to one's performance), or low self-efficacy (belief in one's own capabilities). Again, this is an area where parents may need to seek professional help.

Undetected learning disabilities may be the cause of the problem, so parents always should have that checked out. In some cases, the child's disability may be inhibiting his or her strengths, causing a bright child to look like an underachiever, or simply an average student. Underachievement also may be caused by a lack of educational provisions, which include inappropriate curriculum or a mismatch of instructional style and philosophy of the teacher, in which case parents will want to look carefully at educational options.

Often, there is a combination of causes of underachievement. Work with school personnel and outside professionals to find strategies for working with your underachiever. The first step is to try to figure out the cause. Once that is determined, everyone can work toward a solution for improvement.

PARENT RESOURCES: UNDERACHIEVEMENT

- Rimm, S. B. (2008). *Why bright kids get poor grades and what you can do about it: A six-step program for parents and teachers.* Scottsdale, AZ: Great Potential Press.
- Whitley, M. D. (2001). *Bright minds, poor grades: Understanding and motivating your underachieving child.* New York: Perigee Trade.

Raising a Gifted Child

ECONOMIC AND
CULTURAL DIFFERENCES

Coming from a culture where education is not valued can be very difficult for a bright child. An inadequate school environment just adds to this difficulty. Parents of gifted children have an especially difficult time in these situations. There are choices, however. Some of the strategies you might choose include:

- Find a different school for your child to attend—either public or private. Your district may have an open enrollment policy that allows you to choose a different school, or it may have a magnet school to which your child can apply. Also, don't rule out private schools. Although they may be expensive, they also may offer scholarships.

- Find a mentor for your child—someone who can show your student possibilities outside his own environment and will coach him in ways of getting there. If you don't know someone personally who you can ask, check with school personnel and community organizations like Big Brothers Big Sisters (http://www.bbbs.org) or a nearby religious institution. If your religious institution does not have a program that offers mentoring or tutoring, widen your circle to those institutions outside of your community.

- Fill your house with books and read them to your children often. Books will help your students see the possibilities of life. The supply of books is unlimited if you use your local library.

I meet the most interesting people when traveling. Often this takes place in taxi cabs or shuttles to and from the airport. Recently, I had a taxi cab driver who had a "need to talk." The man entered the United States in 1986 from Eritrea under political asylum. Eritrea is a small African country located on the Red Sea between Sudan and Ethiopia. Mostly, the driver wanted to talk about his children, ages 12 and 14. He was obviously very proud of them and their achievements. Each of the boys was at the top of his class academically. The father said that he and his wife work very hard to provide for their children financially and to instill in them the value of hard work and the importance of education. "After all," he said, "education is the key to success."

Another time I used a "ride share" taxi to get downtown from the airport. It's about half the cost and involves waiting around 5 minutes until the taxi arrangers can find two other people going the same direction who are willing to share the cab. I was sitting in the backseat waiting for the next rider when the door opened and in entered a very good-looking African American man, wearing a handsome navy suit and spit-polished shoes. He was very friendly and introduced himself as Lyndon. After saying "hello," he immediately started working on his Blackberry, alternating the reading of e-mail with making business calls. This went on for 10 or 15 minutes with him moving very quickly from one matter to the next. I grew exhausted just watching and listening to him.

Somewhere along the line, he stopped working and we started a conversation. I was fascinated by his story because it fit so well with the area of gifted education.

Lyndon grew up in a small, poor town in Texas. His parents did not have opportunities to go to college, and I'm not even sure they finished high school. Lyndon's parents were only teenagers when he was born—too young, thought his grandparents—so he was initially raised by the older relatives.

In elementary school, Lyndon was hyperactive and always talking. According to Lyndon's point of view, this caused him to be placed in a resource room for children with learning disabilities. He felt stigmatized. Somewhere along the line, he had a teacher (we'll call her Mrs. Johnson) who looked at him differently. She saw his strengths, not his constant distracting chatter. One day she pulled him aside and said to him, "I'm going to call your mother tonight. I can tell you're a smart boy and I want to have you tested." Through the advocacy of Mrs. Johnson, Lyndon was tested and found to be very bright and was placed in a magnet program for gifted students. Suddenly he saw possibilities outside his immediate environment. He skipped one grade in elementary school while in this magnet program.

When he was in middle school, Lyndon was invited to attend a special program on the East Coast for bright, underprivileged students. This led to him receiving a scholarship for a prep school for 2 years. I asked Lyndon how his parents felt about him going away to school. He said that it was difficult for his mother, but his father was very supportive. When his father was in the military, he had seen that there was "another world out there" and wanted to give his son the opportunity to experience that. After some time, Lyndon missed his friends back home and decided to finish his final years at his old high school. When he returned to that school, he skipped yet another grade.

Lyndon went on to attend Brown University and then got a graduate degree at The University of Chicago. He is now a very successful business executive. All of this happened because he was shown the possibilities of a different life and he had adults who made sure those possibilities could take place.

Lyndon is now married and has two preschoolers. Because of his experiences, he realizes that doors can be opened when one is exposed to the possibilities out there. He is making a concerted effort to give his children even more exposure than he had. He wants them to know many different types of people. He has them in an environment where they are already speaking two languages. He exposes them to lots of books and provides many enriching experiences.

By the way, Mrs. Johnson, the teacher who recognized Lyndon's talents, still remains in his life. She was one of those special teachers who stayed in touch and was a guiding force. Mrs. Johnson "made a difference." She attended his graduations from high school, college, and graduate school. She attended his wedding and the birthday parties of his children. She is a part of his family and a very valued individual.

Eduardo lived with his large family in the barrio. Like his many siblings, he walked every day to the neighborhood school. The school was run down and most of the students struggled, working below grade level. Unlike many of his peers, Eduardo really liked learning. Things seemed to "click" with him, even though he did not received a lot of encouragement from home.

Raising a Gifted Child

One day, when he was in third grade, his teacher introdu
Eduardo to Maria, a high school student who also enjoyed lea
ing. Maria was on a roll and had her sights on finishing high
school and going on to college. She understood that there were
opportunities outside the neighborhood where she was raised.
Maria and Eduardo began meeting on a regular basis and Maria
would tell the younger student about her plans in life. She also
encouraged Eduardo's studies and told him the kinds of classes
he should take as they became available. Maria became Eduardo's mentor—someone who acted as a role model. The boy
eventually not only went on to college, but received a couple of
graduate degrees.

Often one hears stories about people who came from underprivileged backgrounds and were greatly influenced by someone
with a strong interest in their well-being who acted as a role
model. In each of the cases above, there was someone who cared.
This person of influence may be a mentor, a teacher, an uncle,
a parent, or a neighbor. It even could be another student with
a bit more experience. Whoever it is, this caring person shows
the student that there are choices in life.

See Chapter 6 in this book for more information on mentoring and other possibilities for educating your child.

TWICE-EXCEPTIONAL STUDENTS

For many people the terms *learning disability* and *giftedness*
are at opposite ends of a continuum. Many people still believe
that giftedness is equated with outstanding achievement across

all subject areas, but a person truly can be both gifted and have a learning disability. We call these children twice-exceptional or GT/LD.

Children who are gifted and have a learning disability exhibit remarkable talents or strengths in some areas and incapacitating weaknesses in others. These children can be grouped into three categories: those identified as gifted, those identified as learning disabled, and those not recognized as either gifted or learning disabled.

Identified as Gifted

Janet's parents had her evaluated by a psychologist when she was 4. On a widely accepted intelligence test she achieved an IQ score of 140. Her parents assumed that Janet would breeze through school with little effort, but as she advanced through the grades the discrepancies widened between expectations and actual performance.

Janet was very articulate, so her teachers usually were impressed with her ability to share her knowledge verbally. Her spelling and handwriting, however, were atrocious. She also had hard time finishing assignments and getting notes to and from school. Her desk and notebook were a mess. Her teacher and parents were convinced that if she would only try harder, she would succeed.

This group of students is easily identified as gifted because of high achievement or high IQ scores, but as they grow older and school becomes more rigorous, discrepancies widen between expected and actual performance and the student falls considerably behind peers. Because a student may be considered gifted, he is likely to be overlooked for the screening procedures necessary to identify a subtle learning disability. The child's underachievement often is attributed to poor self-concept, lack of motivation, or laziness.

Identified as Having Learning Disabilities

Elizabeth was not doing well academically. She was identified as learning disabled in the first grade. Her parents and teachers focused on her difficulties learning at school. Her self-image was lacking and she was quite disruptive in class. She was frequently off task, did a lot of daydreaming, complained of headaches and stomachaches, and did everything possible to avoid her school work.

Her parents and teachers tended to disregard her high-level interests at home. She had an incredible ability to build complicated structures with Lego bricks, and she had recently started a neighborhood campaign to save endangered animals.

These children are first noticed because of what they cannot do, rather than because of the talent they demonstrate. Parents and teachers tend to focus on the problem, while paying little attention to the student's strengths and interests. Often these children have high-level interests at home showing creativity, intellectual strength, and passion for hobbies. Inadequate assessments and/or a depressed IQ score often lead to an underestimation of intellectual abilities.

Not Recognized as Either Gifted or Learning Disabled

Eight-year-old Pedro was an expert on bugs. He could name and classify a hundred species of insects. He had a huge personal collection that was displayed methodically in boxes all over his room. Narrow pins carefully inserted through the bodies of each insect held them in place in neat rows on Styrofoam. Each insect was categorized according to type and color. Pedro was automatically excluded from consideration for gifted programming at his school because he read only at grade level.

Many educators view below-grade-level achievement as a prerequisite to a diagnosis of a learning disability. An extremely bright student who is struggling to stay on grade level may have developed extraordinary compensation techniques and, therefore, not receive services for learning difficulties because she is not failing. Identification of a subtle disability would help students and adults understand why the student has to work so hard to stay at grade level.

Being twice-exceptional can be very frustrating for parents, teachers, and students—especially if there is a lack of understanding of the subject. Arming oneself with knowledge about the topic will enlighten and, hopefully, lead to coping strategies or modifications in learning techniques. Gifted, learning-disabled children need an environment that will nurture their gifts, attend to their learning disabilities, and provide them with emotional support to deal with their inconsistent abilities.

Remediation of basic skills historically has been the single focus of efforts to serve students once they are classified as learning disabled. Although it is very important to try to remediate basic skills, focusing on weaknesses at the expense of developing gifts can result in poor self-esteem, a lack of motivation, depression, and stress; therefore, in addition to offering remediation, it is essential to focus attention on the development of strengths, interests, and superior intellectual capacities.

Observe the effective methods that your child uses to learn for fun. Incorporate these methods into his school learning as much as possible. Find ways to do work at home that blend with what is happening in the classroom (e.g., if the class is studying dinosaurs, help your child learn about the subject in ways that fit into her own strengths).

Spend time with your twice-exceptional child and focus on activities that accentuate his strong points. Help your young person see that there are things at which she excels. She may never learn how to spell or read quickly, but there are things she can do quite well. Tap into creativity; help her find new ways to get information that do not frustrate efforts.

PARENT RESOURCES: GIFTED AND LEARNING-DISABLED CHILDREN

- *Twice-Exceptional (2e) Newsletter*—http://www.2enewsletter.com
- Vail, P. (1989). *Smart kids with school problems: Things to know and ways to help.* New York: Plume.
- Weinfeld, R., Jeweler, S., Barnes-Robinson, L., & Roffman Shevitz, B. (2006). *Smart kids with learning difficulties: Overcoming obstacles and realizing potential.* Waco, TX: Prufrock Press.

HIGHLY GIFTED

Even in kindergarten, Olaf was a "walking encyclopedia." He was able to read at a 12th-grade level and seemed to remember every fact he came across. Olaf had no intellectual peers in kindergarten. He skipped first grade. He had no intellectual peers in second grade. He had no one who resembled an intellectual peer until high school. Can you imagine how difficult this was for Olaf and his family? He had no one with whom he could relate, and the students in his classes really wanted nothing to do with him. They found him to be a real oddity.

Giftedness is on a continuum. Only a very small number of individuals is highly (a minuscule number profoundly) gifted. Although it may be a challenge to address the needs of gifted students, it is a much greater hurdle to address the needs of the highly or profoundly gifted. This small cohort may be particularly vulnerable, because it is extremely difficult for schools to meet their academic, social, and emotional needs.

These children often have remarkably high scores on individually scored IQ tests. Others may be prodigies in areas such as math, science, language, and/or the arts.

Parents with highly gifted students may consider the following:

- Enrolling their student in a magnet school that is either designed specifically for gifted students or one that has a specific academic focus (i.e., the arts, math and science, or technology).

- Enrolling their child in a specialized school (either a brick-and-mortar or a virtual school) designed for the highly gifted. See the section on Distance Learning in Chapter 6.
- Using grade acceleration, including rapid acceleration (where a student skips more than one grade over his years of school).
- Using early entrance, a strategy that affords the opportunity to start college or university work at younger than normal age—sometimes as early as age 12. See Chapter 6 for more information.
- Finding a mentor who will guide your child in areas of special interest.
- Homeschooling so that the young person is able to move at her own pace and study areas of interest in depth.

If you have a highly gifted student, it is likely that you will need to use a variety of strategies to meet her needs.

PARENT RESOURCES: HIGHLY GIFTED CHILDREN
- The Davidson Institute for Talent Development—http://www.ditd.org

   The Davidson Academy of Nevada is a public school for profoundly gifted students. This Web site includes many articles and a database of resources.
- Gross, M. U. M. (2003). *Exceptionally gifted children.* New York: RoutledgeFalmer.

- The Hollingworth Center for Highly Gifted Children—http://www.hollingworth.org

  This Web site offers written material and Internet resources.
- Colangelo, N., Lupkowski-Shoplik, A., Lipscomb, J., Forstadt, L., & Assouline, S. G. (2002). *Iowa Acceleration Scale manual: A guide for whole-grade acceleration* K–8). Scottsdale, AZ: Great Potential Press.

  This is a tool for determining the appropriateness of whole-grade acceleration.
- *A Nation Deceived: How Schools Hold Back America's Brightest Students*—http://nationdeceived.org

  The entire Templeton National Report on Acceleration, which discusses all types of acceleration, can be downloaded here.
- Kay, K., Robson, D., & Brennerman, J. F. (Eds.). (2007). *High IQ kids: Collected insights, information, and personal stories from the experts.* Minneapolis, MN: Free Spirit.

CONCLUSION

There are many unique subgroups of giftedness, including young children, underachievers, those with economic and cultural differences, twice-exceptional, and highly gifted. Each subgroup requires a different understanding and different approach.

CONCLUSION

SCHOOLS cannot possibly provide a complete education for young people; no one entity can. One's learning comes from both formal education and all experiences outside of school. As a parent, you contribute to this process when you take your children to the library, to cultural events, to museums, and on trips to areas outside their neighborhoods. You help educate kids when you read to them, discuss concepts and ideas with them, encourage their hobbies, enroll them in music lessons, or send them to camp.

I hope you will find the resources in this book helpful as you raise your kids. I also hope you will always ask questions about the education of your children, knowing that it is OK when there are not black and white answers to those questions.

There is not one correct way to educate gifted youngsters; instead, there are many possibilities. Mix and match what works for your family, and understand that your contributions to the educational process are at least as important as any formal education they may receive. Instill in young people the ultimate responsibility for the growth of their own minds. Above all, love and enjoy the family experience.

REFERENCES

Berger, S. L. (2006). *College planning for gifted students: Choosing and getting into the right college.* Waco, TX: Prufrock Press.

Cherry Creek Schools. (n.d.). *Communicating with school: A positive approach.* Retrieved April 24, 2008, from http://www.ccsd.k12.co.us/GT/SupportYourChild

Damron, G. (2006, November 19). Teen goes nuclear: He creates fusion in his Oakland Township home. *Detroit Free Press.* Retrieved April 24, 2008, from http://research.lifeboat.com/teen.goes.nuclear.htm

Dweck, C. (2007). *Mindset: The new psychology of success.* New York: Ballantine Books.

Fertig, C. (2006, April 29). Re: Keep gifted students motivated through mentoring. Message posted to http://resources.prufrock.com/GiftedChildInformationBlog/tabid/57/articleType/ArticleView/articleID/140/Default.aspx

Golon, A. S. (2008). *Visual-spatial learners: Differentiation strategies for creating a successful classroom.* Waco, TX: Prufrock Press.

Goleman, D. (1997). *Emotional intelligence: Why it can matter more than IQ.* New York: Bantam.

Hakim, J. (2002a). *A History of US* (10 Vol. Set). New York: Oxford University Press.

Halsted, J. W. (2002). *Some of my best friends are books: Guiding gifted readers from preschool to high school* (2nd ed.). Scottsdale, AZ: Great Potential Press.

Hakim, J. (2002b). *Freedom: A history of US.* New York: Oxford University Press.

Hess, A. (n.d.). *How to find a mentor.* Retrieved June 30, 2008, from http://www.sciencebuddies.org/mentoring/top_science-fair_mentors.shtml

Machuk, Y. (2006). Prime mentors program. *Understanding Our Gifted, 19*(1), 8–9.

National Geographic. (n.d.). *The five themes of geography.* Retrieved May 2, 2008, from http://www.nationalgeographic.com/resources/ngo/education/themes.html

No Child Left Behind Act, 20 U.S.C. § 6301 (2001).

Siegle, D. (2005). *Developing mentorship programs for gifted students.* Waco, TX: Prufrock Press.

Siemens Foundation. (2007). *2007–08 Siemens competition in math, science & technology.* Retrieved June 30, 2008, from http://www.siemens-foundation.org/en/competition/2007_winners.htm

Strauss, V. (2008, February 18). Relentless questioning paves a deeper path. *The Washington Post.* Retrieved February 20, 2008, from http://www.washingtonpost.com/wp-dyn/content/article/2008/02/17/AR2008021702206.html

Szabos, J. (1989). Bright child/gifted learner. *Challenge Magazine,*
34. Retrieved June 30, 2008, from http://www.tusd.k12.
az.us/CONTENTS/depart/gate/Documents/Handbook.
pdf

Torrance, P. E., Goff, K., & Satterfield, N. B. (1997). *Mul-*
ticultural mentoring of the gifted and talented. Waco, TX:
Prufrock Press.

RESOURCES

THROUGHOUT this book are many resources that are specific to chapter topics. Here are more general resources with which you also will want to become familiar.

GIFTED ASSOCIATIONS AND CONFERENCES

National Association for Gifted Children (NAGC)—http://www.nagc.org

Click on "Gifted by State" to find a list of affiliated state Web sites. Browse not only your own state's Web site, but those of other states. For instance, California has a lot of good resources listed that will be helpful no matter where you live.

Gifted Conferences at Hoagies' Gifted Education Page—http://www.hoagiesgifted.org/conferences.htm

Here you will find a comprehensive list of gifted conferences throughout the world. The list is constantly being updated.

JOURNALS, MAGAZINES, AND NEWSLETTERS

Publications that are marked as scholarly are more technical in nature.

Duke Gifted Letter—http://www.dukegiftedletter.com
    This free online newsletter is filled with practical tools and inspiration for parenting your gifted child.

Gifted Child Quarterly—http://www.nagc.org (click on Publications)
    GCQ publishes original scholarly reviews of literature, research studies, and manuscripts that explore policy.

Gifted Child Today—http://www.prufrock.com (click on Journals & Magazines)
    GCT offers information about teaching and parenting gifted and talented children, including lesson ideas, program suggestions, and new product announcements.

Gifted Education Communicator—http://www.cagifted.org (click on Publications)
    This journal is published by the California Association for the Gifted. Its primary target is parents and educators of K–12 gifted children.

Gifted Education Press Quarterly—http://www.giftededpress.com

Here is an online scholarly publication that provides a resource for developing and advocating for programs for gifted students.

Imagine Magazine—http://cty.jhu.edu/imagine

This magazine is for middle and high school students who want to take control of their learning and get the most out of their precollege years. It provides insights, information, and solid counseling to young, motivated readers and their parents.

Journal for the Education of the Gifted—http://www.prufrock.com (click on Journals & Magazines)

JEG offers scholarly information and research on the educational and psychological needs of gifted and talented children.

Journal of Advanced Academics—http://www.prufrock.com (click on Journals & Magazines)

This is a scholarly publication that focuses on research that supports and enhances advanced academic achievement for students of all ages.

Parenting for High Potential—http://www.nagc.org (click on Publications)

This magazine is for parents who want to develop their children's gifts and talents.

Roeper Review—http://www.roeper.org/RoeperInstitute (Click on *Roeper Review*)

This publication provides scholarly articles that deal with research, observation, experience, theory, and practice as they relate to the growth, emotions, and the education of gifted and talented learners.

2e Twice-Exceptional Newsletter—http://www.2enewsletter.com

This electronic publication promotes understanding of twice-exceptional children and what they need to do their best.

Understanding Our Gifted—http://www.openspacecomm.com (Click on Publications.)

UOG offers practical advice, social and emotional concerns, strategies to use at home and school, and educational options. It is written for parents, educators, and counselors.

WEB SITES

The following Web sites contain large amounts of general and specific information on children with high potential.

Davidson Institute—http://www.ditd.org

The Davidson Institute is a national nonprofit organization dedicated to supporting profoundly gifted students under 18, their parents, and educators. This Web site contains a large collection of information for and about gifted students, their parents, and educators.

Hoagies' Gifted Education Page—http://www.hoagiesgifted.org

This Web site contains articles and links to everything you could ever want to know about gifted education. There are sections for both parents and kids.

Prufrock Press Inc.—http://www.prufrock.com

Click on the link to Parenting Gifted Children and find access to numerous articles of interest and also two gifted education blogs.

Supporting Emotional Needs of the Gifted (SENG)—http://www.sengifted.org

SENG draws attention to the unique emotional needs of gifted children. An online library of articles is available, as well as information about parent support groups.

ADDITIONAL RESOURCES BY CHAPTER

Chapter 2

Adderholdt, M., & Goldberg, J. (1999). *Perfectionism: What's bad about being too good?* Minneapolis, MN: Free Spirit.

Delisle, J., & Galbraith, J. (2002). *When gifted kids don't have all the answers.* Minneapolis, MN: Free Spirit.

Galbraith, J. (2000). *You know your child is gifted when . . . : A beginner's guide to life on the bright side.* Minneapolis, MN: Free Spirit.

Greenspon, T. S. (2001). *Freeing our families from perfectionism.* Minneapolis, MN: Free Spirit.

Greenspon, T. S. (2007). *What to do when good enough isn't good enough: The real deal on perfectionism: A guide for kids.* Minneapolis, MN: Free Spirit.

Matthews, D. J., & Foster, J. F. (2004). *Being smart about gifted children: A guidebook for parents and educators.* Scottsdale, AZ: Great Potential Press.

Strip, C. A. (2000). *Helping gifted children soar: A practical guide for parents and teachers.* Scottsdale, AZ: Great Potential Press.

Chapter 3

Study Guides and Strategies—http://www.studygs.net

This site contains organizational tools for school, divided into categories such as studying, reading skills, and preparing for tests.

Study Skills Self-Help Information—http://www.ucc.vt.edu/stdysk/stdyhlp.html

This site contains time management strategies, strategies for reading nonfiction material, and note taking.

Cohen, L. M., & Frydenberg, E. (2006). *Coping for capable kids: Strategies for parents, teachers, and students.* Waco, TX: Prufrock Press.

Cross, T. L. (2005). *The social and emotional lives of gifted kids: Understanding and guiding their development.* Waco, TX: Prufrock Press.

Delisle, J. R. (2006). *Parenting gifted kids: Tips for raising happy and successful children.* Waco, TX: Prufrock Press.

Chapter 4

Chessville—http://www.chessville.com

Oklahoma Scholastic Chess Organization—http://www.okschess.org/starting

U.S. Chess Federation—http://main.uschess.org

Wikipedia: List of Hobbies—http://en.wikipedia.org/wiki/List_of_hobbies

Yahoo Directory of Recreational Hobbies—http://dir.yahoo.com/Recreation/Hobbies

Olenchak, F. R. (1998). *They say my kid's gifted: Now what?* Waco, TX: Prufrock Press.

Roberts, J. (2005). *Enrichment opportunities for gifted learners.* Waco, TX: Prufrock Press.

Sayler, M. (1997). *Raising champions: A parent handbook for nurturing gifted children.* Waco, TX: Prufrock Press.

Chapter 5

Creative Thinking Techniques—http://www.virtualsalt.com/crebook2.htm

Creative Problem Solving—http://ceo.binghamton.edu/kowalik/docs/CreativeProblemSolving.pdf

Tools for Creating Ideas—http://creatingminds.org/tools/tools_ideation.htm

Draze, D. (2005). *Primarily problem solving: Creative problem solving activities.* Waco, TX: Prufrock Press.

Eberle, B., & Stanish, B. (1996). *CPS for kids: A resource book for teaching creative problem-solving to children.* Waco, TX: Prufrock Press.

Elwell, P. A. (1993). *CPS for teens: Classroom activities for teaching creative problem solving.* Waco, TX: Prufrock Press.

Treffinger, D. J. (2000). *Practice problems for creative problem solving.* Waco, TX: Prufrock Press.

Chapter 7

Assouline, S., & Lupkowski-Shoplik, A. (2005). *Developing math talent: A guide for educating gifted and advanced learners in math.* Waco, TX: Prufrock Press.

Bossé, M. J., & Rotigel, J. V. (2006). *Encouraging your child's math talent: The involved parents' guide.* Waco, TX: Prufrock Press.

Chapter 8

Fisher, G. L., Cummings, R., & Urbanovic, J. (2002). *The survival guide for kids with LD.* Minneapolis, MN: Free Spirit.

Matthews, M. S. (2006). *Gifted English language learners.* Waco, TX: Prufrock Press.

Olszewski-Kubilius, P. (2003). *Early gifts: Recognizing and nurturing children's talents.* Waco, TX: Prufrock Press.

Saunders, J. (1991). *Bringing out the best: A guide for parents of young gifted children.* Minneapolis, MN: Free Spirit.

Weinfeld, R., Barnes-Robinson, L., Jeweler, S., & Roffman Shevitz, B. (2006). *Smart kids with learning difficulties: Overcoming obstacles and realizing potential.* Waco, TX: Prufrock Press.

ABOUT THE AUTHOR

CAROL Fertig has worked in the field of education for more than 35 years and has been a gifted education resource to parents, teachers, and administrators for more than 20 years. She has a master's degree in educational psychology/gifted education and has served as a classroom teacher, gifted education specialist, speaker, consultant, and staff developer. She has written numerous articles that have appeared in journals, magazines, and on the Internet. Currently Carol is the editor of *Understanding Our Gifted* and also writes the Gifted Children Information Blog located on the Prufrock Press Web site.